Accounting & Finance

Accounting & Finance in Practice

Leslie Chadwick MBA, FCCA, Cert. Ed.

Stanley Thornes (Publishers) Ltd

First published in 1990 by:
Stanley Thornes (Publishers) Ltd
Old Station Drive
Leckhampton
CHELTENHAM GL53 0DN
England

British Library Cataloguing in Publication Data

Chadwick, Leslie
  Accounting and finance in practice.
  1. Business. Accounting
  I. Title
  658.15

  ISBN 0–7487–0402–7

Typeset by Wyvern Typesetting, Bristol
Printed and bound in Great Britain at The Bath Press, Avon

Contents

Preface

The principal aim of this book is to provide readings which are *readable, interesting, relevant* and *practical*.

It is designed for use on a wide range of Accountancy and Business Studies courses ranging from BEC HNC/HND courses; first- and second-year degree courses; MBA courses; professional accountancy courses, and it aims at providing a wide range of readings which it is hoped can be used to develop the comprehensional skills of the reader. Lecturers and professional tutors should find it particularly helpful in providing comprehensional material to support courses which involve a lot of 'number crunching'.

Although many of the articles in this book aim at addressing the problems of the real world of business, they do include numerous useful references to the literature on the subject. This makes the book of particular value to those students who are involved in the writing of projects and dissertations. It could, in fact, provide the starting point for many projects and be of great use when carrying out a literature search.

Many of the articles should appeal to qualified accountants and managers, not only for continuing education purposes but also because they contain highly relevant information; information and strategies which could save lots of money.

All of the articles which are reproduced in this book were written by my co-authors and myself. Many of these articles were written to fill gaps in existing literature and they include real-life examples.

Leslie Chadwick

About the author

Leslie Chadwick MBA, FCCA, Cert. Ed.

Leslie Chadwick commenced his professional career in 1958 with a lengthy spell in local government with the Huddersfield Passenger Transport. He qualified as a Certified Accountant in 1965 and in 1966 moved into industry, spending two years as a Management Accountant with Holset Engineering, manufacturers of turbochargers, fan drives and couplings, etc. This was followed by two years in public practice with a firm of Chartered Accountants.

He became a Lecturer/Senior Lecturer in Accountancy at Huddersfield Polytechnic in 1971 before taking up his present appointment as a Lecturer in Accounting and Financial Management at the University of Bradford Management Centre in 1978. Since his appointment at the University of Bradford, he has been a regular contributor to many of the UK's leading professional journals. He has, to date, published numerous articles and a number of books, one of the most recent being *Creative Cost and Management Accounting* with Michael Magin (Hutchinson, 1989). He was invited to be responsible for the accountancy, marketing and management terminology in the recently published *Pan Dictionary of Economics and Business*.

His research interests are: Small Business Finance, Working Capital Management, Value for Money Auditing, and Retail and Distribution Management.

Acknowledgements

The author and publishers would like to express their thanks to the following journals for their permission to reproduce the articles which appear in this book:

Certified Accountants Students' Newsletter
Certified Accountant
Accountancy
Management Accounting
Journal of the Institute of Bankers
The Accountant
Retail and Distribution Management
Management Services
Building Technology and Management
Accountants Weekly
Management and Control of Capital in Industry (book published by the CIMA)
Accountancy Age

Also, the author would like to thank his co-authors for their contribution towards the articles that have been included in this book. They are: Christopher Metalle, David Ward, Ken Tonkin, Alan Waddington, Keith Pickles, Janek Ratnatunga, Duncan Aspinall, Deborah Rogers and Bruce Thew.

Accountancy

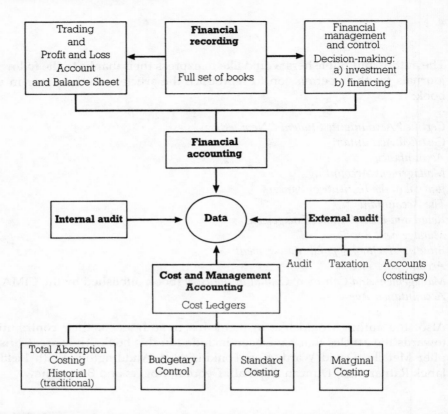

Accounting systems involve the use of the basic data or information in different ways, i.e. cost information can be used in a variety of ways to produce quite different statements.

Financial accounting has two basic aims – leading to Trading and Profit and Loss Account and Balance Sheet–overall picture.

Cost accounting – *traditional* is an extension of Financial Accounting, giving more detail of economic performance of firm, departments, jobs, etc., but still basically historical.

– *modern* is designed to assist management in planning its economic performance, controlling costs and improving profitability.

Management accounting is a modern term covering the use of all accounting techniques, particularly those of modern costing, for the guidance of management in the improvement of the firm's economic performance.

1

Sources of business finance and financial structure

This chapter commences with a quick review of the principal sources of business finance, with a special emphasis on those that can be obtained from external sources. However, the importance of retained earnings is not overlooked. Although internal sources of finance are mentioned, it should be noted that it is covered in greater depth in Chapter 4 under the heading 'Working capital management'. The area of financial structure and capital structure receives an introductory treatment in the second reading. This should be of value to those readers who are at the start of their studies in this area.

The financial management topic of dividend policy was specially written for those readers who have not yet come across this 'puzzle'. The approach taken is for the reader to imagine that they can listen into a board room conversation as the directors discuss their ideas on dividend policy. A running commentary is provided, which assesses the validity of their comments. The reader should, it is hoped, find this to be a useful introduction to the subject.

The growth of the venture capital market and the development of corporate venturing should be of interest to students, qualified accountants and general management. The area of corporate venturing is one which is particularly new to the UK and an area in which there is a shortage of UK literature.

Sources of capital

In everyday life capital is frequently used to describe money, but to the accountant capital means much more.[1] To the accountant capital employed includes:

- share capital
- retained profits
- loans and debentures, and
- working capital.

The businessperson may well ask the question, 'Why is capital shown with the liabilities in the Balance Sheet? I thought it was my principal asset.' The answer to this question is that capital is an amount invested in the business by the proprietor, shareholder or other third party, and it does therefore represent a claim on the assets. Capital is increased by the portion of periodic income which is retained, i.e. ploughed back profits.

Queries

Question   Where do I go to obtain capital?
Answer   A multitude of places, the list is endless.

Question   Which type of capital do I need?
Answer   It all depends upon how much you want and for how long you want it.

Question   How much will it cost me to borrow the money?
Answer   This will vary with each particular source, but one thing that is certain is that the charges will reflect the time span of the finance and the risk to the institution making the finance available. Remember that in addition to paying interest on loans that there is also an obligation to repay the capital.

Question   How do I decide upon how long I need the capital for?
Answer   One way of doing this is to look at what you're using the capital for and matching it to the life of the asset or project.

Matching finance

The notion of matching the type of finance with the life of an asset or duration of a project is of practical application. The repayments of the capital and interest are being made out of the additional income supposedly generated as a result of employing the asset or taking on the project, e.g. company cars, which are to be replaced say every two or three years, could well be financed from short-term sources.

Short-term sources of capital (up to 3 years)

Short-term capital can be utilised to provide cover for fluctuations in working capital, the financing of short-lived assets and transactions which are self-financing in the short term.

Bank overdrafts from the clearing banks and merchant banks offer a very flexible source of capital which is ideal for assisting in providing working capital. It must be noted, however, that a certain proportion of the working capital should be regarded as a fixed investment and financed from long-term sources of funds. Amounts can be repaid or withdrawn as and when appropriate. If the concern requires more on overdraft an increase can be negotiated quite speedily with the bank. In some cases the banks may ask for security or a guarantee.

Short-term loans are usually granted by the clearing banks and merchant banks for a particular purpose. The capital and interest is usually repaid in instalments at regular intervals. The interest charges may be fixed or variable. Depending upon the amount and the size and track record of the company concerned, the bank may require security.

It is worth noting that what is short-term, medium-term and long-term will in practice depend upon the nature of the industry and the size of the company.

Trade credit
One of the most frequently used sources of short-term finance is the trade credit provided by the suppliers of goods and services.

> It is said,
> That honest Ed,
> Buys goods on 90 days' credit,
> In that time,
> He sells them all, and
> that's how he makes a profit.[2]

The time lag between the receipt of the goods and payment for them allows the company purchasing those goods to process/sell some or all of them. It is imperative that a company maintains a good working relationship with its suppliers. The support of sympathetic creditors in times of cash flow problems could prove vital to the survival of the company.

However, where cash discounts are offered for prompt payment, this should not be ignored. It must be remembered that a discount of, say, $2\frac{1}{2}$ per cent for payment within seven days of the invoice where normal settlement is, say, 45 days from the invoice date amounts to a substantial effective annual rate of interest of around 24 per cent!

Bridging loans
These are usually used to cover the period between the exchange of contracts and the completion date for transactions involving the purchase or sale of property. The financial institutions tend to charge a rate of interest which is slightly higher than the rate that they charge on overdrafts and may also require an arrangement fee.

Invoice discounting
Here, the Invoice Discounting Companies, for a fee, will advance immediately around 75 to 80 per cent of the invoice value. When the company receives payment from the debtors concerned the discounting company will be paid. Note that the client business is still responsible for collecting the debts relating to invoices discounted.

Factoring

In contrast to invoice discounting, the factoring companies undertake to be responsible for the collection of the debts. The company sells its debtors at a discount to the factor who may advance the money immediately or at the date on which the customer would have settled his account. The contract may be without recourse (i.e. the factor assumes full responsibility for collecting the debt) or with recourse. The greater the risk to the factor the greater the fees that will be charged. Factoring may also include the provision of sales ledger accounting and credit control procedures.

'Accounts receivable' financing

It is possible to arrange with certain financial institutions, such as merchant banks, hire purchase companies, etc., for them to provide a company with cash on a continuing basis by pledging debtors as security. As with invoice discounting, it is the company's responsibility to collect the debts.

Bills of exchange

The clearing banks, merchant banks, accepting houses and discount houses are all in the business of discounting bills of exchange. The seller of the goods and services drafts the bill, gets the purchaser to accept it, and then on its return from the purchaser the seller is able to obtain immediate payment by discounting the bill. The periods covered by bills of exchange tend to be from around 60 to 180 days. The use of this type of finance does help a business to convert a sale into cash very quickly after the goods have been despatched. Charges will depend to a great extent upon the reputation of the buyer. Specialist advice in drawing up a bill is available from the institutions who deal in this specialised type of finance.

Hire purchase

This tends to be quite an expensive method of buying assets. One must look very carefully at the effective rates of interest which are being charged. One must also be prepared to shop around. Some vendors may offer subsidised rates which may work out less expensive than short-term bank loans. (See also medium-term.)

Proposed dividends and accrued taxation

These are also valuable sources of short-term finance in that the company has the use of those funds for a particular period of time.

Local and central government

The schemes are numerous, various and voluminous and one could write a book on this one aspect of financing. The offerings are constantly changing in name and shape. The accountant/financial manager should therefore ensure that he or she is up to date by obtaining information at regular intervals.

There are grants available for selected industries, e.g. hotels, tourism, manufacturing, small engineering, farming, microprocessing, microelectronics, software, computers, robotics, office and service industries, etc.

Quite a number of firms can receive grants towards the cost of new buildings, plant and equipment if they are for use in designated Development and Special Development Areas.

Where can we obtain information about grants?

A useful publication *Raising Finance – The Guardian Guide For The Small Business* by Clive Woodcock, published by Kogan Page, contains six pages of useful addresses relating to government sources of finance. Then there is the Department of Industry, local authorities, Chambers of Commerce and Regional Development Grant Offices.

Medium-term sources of capital (3–10 years)

This type of finance is used mainly for providing additional working capital or for the purchase of fixed assets such as plant and machinery, fixtures and fittings, and office equipment, which have medium-term lives. Thus, the term of the finance is matched to the life of the asset, project or business venture. They may be also used for re-financing, e.g. converting the hard-core debt of an overdraft into a term loan.

Medium-term loans

A vast proportion of funds employed by manufacturing industry are now taken in the form of medium-term loans, quite probably as a direct result of the matching process. There are several sources from which this type of funding can be obtained, the principal ones being:

- the clearing banks
- merchant banks
- finance houses
- foreign banks, etc.

The terms relating to interest charges and repayment vary considerably, providing the borrower with greater flexibility. Repayments can be scheduled in a number of ways, e.g.

a) Monthly, quarterly or half-yearly.
b) No repayments at all for the first one or two years, i.e. a 'repayment holiday'.
c) Interest only with the capital being repaid at the end of the term.

Such loans may be secured or unsecured depending upon the company's track record, e.g. profitability, size, credit worthiness and market expectations. The rates of interest charged are frequently linked to the LIBOR, i.e. the London Inter-Bank Offered Rate.

The company concerned may lose some degree of control over its affairs in that it may have to supply the financial institution concerned with information on a regular basis, e.g. cash flows, investment plans, etc.

5

The loan guarantee scheme

This scheme was introduced on 1 June 1981. Under this scheme the government undertakes to guarantee a certain proportion of medium-term loans of two to seven years made by the participating financial institutions, e.g. the clearing banks. This scheme was introduced to help the sole traders, partnerships, co-operatives and limited companies of the UK small business sector.

The business expansion scheme

The Business Start-up Scheme was introduced by the Finance Act 1981 as an entirely new tax incentive to attract individuals into taking an equity stake in a new enterprise. This scheme was extended and improved by the Finance Act 1983 and re-named The Business Expansion Scheme.

Venture capital

Venture loans are available from the clearing banks, the ICFC, and certain large companies. They have developed to meet the need for start-up, expansion and development financing. The offerings, terms and conditions do vary and are quite likely to change from time to time. One is therefore advised to contact the institutions concerned when contemplating a need for this particular type of finance.

Other medium-term sources of capital

Debentures may be secured by fixed or floating charge. They appeal to investors who require a relatively risk-free fixed return investment, e.g. Pension Funds. The risk to the company is increased because of the obligation to pay the interest irrespective of whether or not the company makes a profit.

Leasing is provided by leasing companies, finance houses, etc. It frees a company from having to find and repay a lump sum for a fixed asset, e.g. machinery, office furniture and equipment. It can be argued that leasing of fixed assets does provide the company with a hedge against obsolescence, e.g. at the end of the lease a new and improved asset may be leased. The amounts paid for leasing machinery, furniture and equipment are allowable deductions in computing profits for tax purposes. Costs and conditions vary and terms tend to favour around the five year mark.

Hire purchase is usually used to buy a fixed asset, e.g. vehicles, fixtures and machinery. Hire purchase finance is provided by finance houses (a number of whom are subsidiaries of the clearing banks). The instalments paid at regular intervals (could be over the life of the assets, i.e. 'matching') are made up of capital and interest. It is important when assessing the cost of buying an asset on HP that the tax implications are clearly understood.

The EC – an exchange risk agreement was signed in February 1981 with Finance for Industry Ltd, which will assist them to make European Investment Bank (EIB) and European Coal and Steel Community (ECSC) loans available to small manufacturing firms in the Assisted Areas and steel closure areas at attractive rates of interest. In April 1981 a further agreement was signed with the Midland Bank which will assist them to make EIB foreign currency loans available to small firms. Other clearing banks and financial institutions have also negotiated with ECSC for similar agencies to provide loans.

Project loans for specific projects may have their repayment profiles linked to the cash flows expected from the project. These are available from the 'Money Market' made up of accepting houses, UK and overseas banks.

Call loans are available from the 'Money Market' and enable the company to repay tranches of the loan during its life and to redraw as required.

Long-term sources of capital (over 10 years)

Long-term sources of finance can be used to provide long-term assets, e.g. buildings, for the purchase of investments, shares in a subsidiary and for the provision of the 'permanent' working capital.

Equity finance

This represents the ordinary shares which may be issued to shareholders, e.g. via the Stock Exchange to individual or institutional investors. There are a number of classes of ordinary shares with different rights as defined by a company's memorandum and articles of association. The Companies Act 1981/89 gives companies the power to issue redeemable ordinary shares, provided that certain conditions are complied with.

Calls – share capital which has not yet been called up gives a company the added flexibility as to the amount and the timing of future inflows from this source. It should be remembered that once all the cash has been received from an issue of shares, that the buying and selling of those shares on the open market does not provide any new finance for the company whose shares are being sold.

Long-term loans
Provided by:

- the clearing banks
- merchant banks
- finance houses, etc.

Syndicated loans are available via the 'Money Market' and have been developed to provide the huge amounts required by multinational companies and public corporations. *A number of banks come together to provide the facility with the syndicate leader*.

The terms relating to repayment of capital and interest are varied and again the company may have to surrender some of its independence, e.g. a loan with strings attached such as the provision of information, the provision of security, and the vetting of investment plans, etc.

Mortgage loans with repayment periods ranging from around 10 to over 30 years are available from insurance companies, finance houses and pension funds.

Sale and lease back
This highly specialised type of finance usually involves the sale of land and buildings to an insurance company which are then leased back for a term of

years, e.g. 25 years. This method enables an organisation to provide the large amount needed to finance, say, the construction of a new building.

Government sources
As mentioned earlier, there are numerous governmental sources of finance which are essentially long-term.

EC
Funds are also available from the EC from the European Investment Bank (EIB) and the European Coal and Steel Community (ECSC).

Retained profits

One of the major sources of UK business finance is the profits that are 'ploughed back' and invested in the business in the form of working capital and assets.

It should be noted that growth, e.g. in terms of turnover, and profitability do not always go hand in hand. In the UK, one of the most important sources of capital is the retained profits (i.e. undistributed profits). Companies must plough back profits in order to invest in new fixed assets, working capital, external investments and research and development, so as to secure their long term progression and survival.

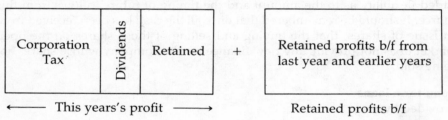

The retained profit may be in the form of the Profit and Loss Account, balance and/or general reserve; either way it has been ploughed back to self-generate company growth.

In the situation where the directors' dividend policy is to have a low dividend payout and a high ploughback, the ordinary shareholders should be compensated for this by the capital growth in the value of their shares.

Internal finance

In addition to the finance provided by ploughing back profits and selling off surplus assets, management may be able to generate additional finance simply by improving the efficiency of the various business functions.

There is a great tendency when finance is required for a particular asset or project to look immediately to external sources. Companies, however, do have hidden sources of finance which can improve their cash flow, e.g. surplus assets, improved stock control, improved credit control, etc.

All branches of management should be concerned with improving the productivity of the capital employed. It is therefore of prime importance that all business functions work together in peace and harmony.

References
[1]Chadwick, L. and Pike, R. *Management and Control of Capital in Industry* (CIMA, 1985).
[2]Written by Leslie Chadwick, inspired by the story of 'Honest Ed', the man who re-opened the Old Vic Theatre in 1983.

Financial structure

The financial structure reflects how a company has financed its assets. This structure will have been determined by management, but constrained by the amounts which the providers of finance are willing to advance. It is also affected by the characteristics of the particular industry and conditioned by the financial structures of other firms within that industry. Thus, the essence of the financial structure is the proportion of each source of finance to the total of the financing mix and the risks and costs associated with that mix (see Fig. 1.1).

What is capital structure?

Capital structure may be described as the more permanent/long-term financing used, such as ordinary shares, preference shares, long-term debt, and reserves (see Fig. 1.1).

Capital structure is not just an array of long-term financing, but also a system of risks and costs associated with each source.

One of the primary objectives of managing the financial and/or capital structure is to ascertain the financing mix which maximises the market value of the company. The cost, therefore, of a firm's existing structure is of great importance. A factor of considerable interest when examining any balance sheet will be the volume and proportion of long-term debt to the equity (i.e. gearing).

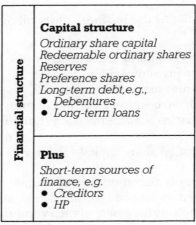

Fig. 1.1 *The components of financial structure*

Gearing and leverage

'Leverage' is used in the United States to describe what in the UK is known as gearing. However, leverage is also a term that, over the years, has gained acceptance in the UK.

Why use gearing? Gearing refers to the relationship between equity (i.e. ordinary share capital plus reserves) and fixed and variable interest bearing securities, e.g., preference shares, debentures and long-term loans. Nowadays, a vast proportion of the long term loans which are taken out, are at variable rates of interest.

If the proportion of fixed and variable interest securities is high the structure is described as being high geared. As the proportion of debt increases (higher gearing) so financial risk will increase and investors (whether of debt or equity) will only be willing to invest in that company if they are recompensed with an adequate return on their investment. If the proportion of fixed and variable interest securities is low, the structure is described as being low geared.

In the real world, what is regarded as high or low depends upon the type of industry, e.g. a firm could appear to be highly geared on paper but low geared when compared with other firms in the same industry.

The idea behind gearing is to provide extra capital upon which additional earnings can be made and thereby boost the returns of the ordinary shareholders, although only if the earnings exceed the cost of the finance which has been used.

Warning: Additional risk to the company which uses gearing manifests itself as an obligation to make fixed and variable interest payments and to repay the capital whether or not the company makes a profit (e.g. debentures). When hard times come along, it is the highly geared companies that are the most vulnerable.

Equity capital

Equity capital is the stake in the business of its ultimate owners. It is comprised of:

- the capital which was originally subscribed for the formation of the company (including share premium), plus
- any further capital issues made since, plus
- any amounts which have been set aside out of profits as reserves, plus
- any profits which have been made but not yet distributed.

Equity capital = issued share capital + reserves + retained profits

Subject to the directors' discretion in distributing dividends, the equity shareholders are entitled to surplus earnings after all prior demands have been satisfied, and to the surplus assets upon a winding up of their company. It is, therefore, more risky but potentially more profitable.

Long-term debt

Debt capital consists of the long-term loans and debentures which have been advanced to the business. The two significant features of debt from the providers' point of view are:

a) the right to a fixed or variable amount of interest per period, which has seniority over dividends and
b) the right to a return of a fixed sum at some future date or upon a winding up of the company, which has seniority over the return of equity capital to investors.

Debt, then, has rights of seniority in two respects over the equity capital, and this makes it less risky than equity.

Thus, there is *additional risk* to the company which arises as a consequence of the legal obligation to pay interest in agreed amounts by stated dates (and repay the capital as and when due) and also the possibility of pledging certain assets as security.

Medium/long-term loans

Medium/long-term loans may be secured by fixed/floating charge.

With debentures there could well be less freedom to manage assets, e.g. the Trustee for the debenture holders is controlled by statute and cannot delay action against a defaulter, whereas with Unsecured Loan Stock it may be possible to arrange to delay/revise action.

The equity capital carries no prescriptive right to a dividend, hence if there is insufficient profit, the dividend can be forgone. Interest on debt is an annual charge, which must be met whether the company makes a profit or not. In times of low or no profit, the company with debt capital will run the risk of being made bankrupt through an inability to meet debt interest. This is called financial risk.

Because debt is a less risky investment from the lender's point of view (initially at least) it tends to be cheaper than equity.

Convertible loan stock reduces the risk to the firm's solvency, as and when the holders convert into equity. This is because the obligation to pay interest and repay the original capital no longer exists.

The bank overdraft and gearing

Many companies now use their bank overdraft as a long-term source of funds. If this is the case, the bank overdraft ought really to be taken into account in the gearing calculation. One such ratio which recognises this fact is the Murphy Prussman Gearing which is calculated as follows:

$$\frac{\text{Debentures} + \text{Loans} + \text{Bank overdraft}}{\text{Total long-term financing including bank overdraft}}$$

11

However, the real truth of the matter is that a bank overdraft will consist of two elements (see Fig. 1.2), namely:

a) an amount which is hard-core debt, and
b) a flexible element.

Fig. 1.2 *The truth about overdrafts*

The advocates against the inclusion of the bank overdraft in gearing calculations point out that a bank overdraft is repayable on demand. My reply to them would be a quite simple question. Would a banker really try to kill off a good customer by calling in their overdraft?

Hire purchase, leasing and gearing

Why use hire purchase? Hire purchase is expensive!

Companies use hire purchase usually to finance short-term fixed assets, e.g. to purchase a motor vehicle over three years. Competitive rates may make the cost of hire purchase cheaper than a bank loan. However, HP is now becoming available for longer terms and may also have to be taken into account when making gearing calculations.

Finance from creditors

Note that creditors represent an interest-free source of capital to the extent that the company can finance itself from them on a continuous basis.

The debt versus equity saga

The proportion of debt raises a gearing problem in that the fixed and variable interest payments take a big slice out of company profits. It is the obligation to pay interest capital in agreed amounts by stated dates or to repay the capital when the debt matures that puts the company to additional risk. If the company has had to provide security for the debt, this further increases the risk undertaken by the shareholders. A debt-free company is considered to be more likely to attract new capital when it is required.

A capital structure which includes some debentures usually means some loss of control and less freedom to manage assets. The trustees for the debenture holders are controlled by statute and cannot delay taking action against a defaulter. With a bank loan, on the other hand, it may be possible to arrange a compromise and reschedule the debt.

If a company issues more ordinary shares this could mean some loss of control, which explains the reluctance on the part of certain boards of directors towards this option. However, is it better to have partial control of a company that is growing than total control of a company that is stagnating?

There is a saying that debt may be used to boost the returns available to the ordinary shareholder. It can be observed from a study of the specially simplified example contained in Table 1 that this statement is a little misleading. In fact, it all depends upon the economic conditions at the time, the rate of interest payable and the rates of taxation.

Table 1 does illustrate quite clearly that in times of recession it is the more highly geared companies that make the lower returns for their equity shareholders. In the case of Structure C, the obligation to make fixed interest payments causes the company to make a loss when conditions are poor or very poor. However, when trading conditions are good or very good, the returns to the ordinary shareholder increase quite significantly when compared with Structure A. If the tax rate was reduced to, say, 40 per cent the returns for the ordinary shareholders would increase as shown in Table 2.

What factors must be taken into account in the planning of a capital structure? Many questions must be answered such as:

a) How much capital is needed? This will be determined by carefully budgeting the value of the fixed assets required immediately and in the future. The amount of working capital also needs to be assessed as a large proportion should be financed from long-term sources. A percentage of the working capital should be regarded as a fixed investment because capital is tied up permanently. Certain minimum levels of stocks and debtors always have to be financed.

b) When is it needed? The preparation of a cash flow forecast (i.e. cash budget) is a great help in the process of assessing financing needs in the short-term. The long-term budgets should help to pinpoint the future funding needed to finance capital expenditure.

c) What is the purpose of the capital structure?

d) How risky is the proposed investment? Will the risk to the company increase and if so why? Careful attention must be paid to the risk/return associated with the company's projects. Assessment of the situation which may arise if things go wrong should not be ignored.

e) Which type of finance should be used?

   The purpose for which the finance is required can certainly assist in determining the type of finance required. However, there are several other factors which merit careful consideration:

   i) *Share capital*. The amount of the authorised and issued share capital, e.g. has the company any calls which it could make?

   ii) *Control*. Would a new issue of ordinary shares mean a loss of control? If debt was used, what restrictions would be placed upon the company? There could be restrictions on other borrowing, the vetting of future investment plans and less freedom to manage the assets.

   iii) *Security*. The quantity and quality of a firm's assets can influence the amount of debt which it may obtain.

Table 1: Returns for ordinary shareholders under various gearing and economic conditions

	Economic conditions				
	Very poor £000	Poor £000	Normal £000	Good £000	Very good £000
Earnings before interest and tax	24	28	32	44	56
STRUCTURE A Gearing factor 0%					
Earnings	24	28	32	44	56
Less interest @ 10%	—	—	—	—	—
Earnings after interest	24	28	32	44	56
Less Taxation (say 50%)	12	14	16	22	28
Available for ordinary shareholders	12	14	16	22	28
% return on ordinary shares	3	3.5	4	5.5	7
STRUCTURE B Gearing factor 50%					
Earnings	24	28	32	44	56
Less interest @ 10%	20	20	20	20	20
Earnings after interest	4	8	12	24	36
Less Taxation (say 50%)	2	4	6	12	18
Available for ordinary shareholders	2	4	6	12	18
% return on ordinary shares	1	2	3	6	9
STRUCTURE C Gearing factor 75%					
Earnings	24	28	32	44	56
Less interest @ 10%	30	30	30	30	30
Earnings after interest	−6	−2	2	14	26
Less Taxation (say 50%)	*−3	*−1	1	7	13
Available for ordinary shareholders	−3	−1	1	7	13
% return on ordinary shares	—	—	1	7	13
STRUCTURE A	£000	£000	£000	£000	£000
Ordinary share capital	400	400	400	400	400
Long-term debt	—	—	—	—	—
STRUCTURE B	£000	£000	£000	£000	£000
Ordinary share capital	200	200	200	200	200
Long-term debt	200	200	200	200	200
STRUCTURE C	£000	£000	£000	£000	£000
Ordinary share capital	100	100	100	100	100
Long-term debt	300	300	300	300	300

*= refund.

Table 2: Tax rate 40%

	Economic conditions				
	Very poor £000	Poor £000	Normal £000	Good £000	Very good £000
STRUCTURE A 0% *Gearing*					
Earnings after interest (*see* Table 1)	24	28	32	44	56
Less Taxation (say 40%)	9.6	11.2	12.8	17.6	22.4
	14.4	16.8	19.2	26.4	33.6
% return on ordinary shares	3.6	4.2	4.8	6.6	8.4
STRUCTURE B 50% *Gearing*					
Earnings after interest (*see* Table 1)	4	8	12	24	36
Less Taxation (say 40%)	1.6	3.2	4.8	9.6	14.4
	2.4	4.8	7.2	14.4	21.6
% return on ordinary shares	1.2	2.4	3.6	7.2	10.8

Note: The returns/losses in Structure C would follow a similar pattern.

Source: Management and Control of Capital in Industry – see Recommended reading.

iv) *Track record*. A satisfactory record of company performance in terms of profitability, liquidity and sales growth has a bearing on the company's ability to attract funds.

v) *Cost*. The cost, taking into account the effects of taxation, must be calculated for each proposed source of funds.

vi) *The current financial structure* cannot be ignored. Higher gearing may discourage other investors from providing funds and increase the possibility of bankruptcy. When trading conditions are adverse, highly geared companies are more likely to go out of business because of having to make high interest payments.

f) What are the important relationships like? The attitudes of the providers of funds, e.g. shareholders and bankers, should be taken into account. It is essential that financial managers establish a good working relationship between themselves and the providers of their funds.

g) Is there sales/earnings stability? A company which has stability in sales and earnings is in a position to take on more debt than a company whose sales and earnings are liable to violent fluctuations.

h) What is the structure of the industry in terms of assets, competition, etc?

i) What will be the effect of current decisions on future market reputation?

j) What are the conversion provisions? Debentures and loan stock with conversion provisions reduce the risk to the company when the holders convert.

k) What is the external environment like? The external environment in which

15

the firm operates must be the subject of constant monitoring. Changes, in the political, economic, social, technological or in factor and product markets, may influence the composition of the capital and financial structure.

Where a company's sales and earnings are growing at a satisfactory rate, its ordinary shares will tend to command a high price. The issue of more ordinary shares at a premium may be desirable. The company must therefore carefully weigh the benefits of using debt against broadening its equity base.

Investors are usually willing to lend funds so long as they are confident that they will make a satisfactory return on their investment and that their capital is secure. Investors other than the ordinary shareholders also like to see adequate equity participation – if you are not prepared to risk your money, why should I risk mine?

The environment in which firms have to operate makes it impossible to lay down clear cut guidelines because the basic assumptions upon which they were founded may change overnight. There are no easy decisions in the world of business finance, just trade-offs!

Assessing the financial structure

A factor of interest in all balance sheets is the volume and proportion of debt to other assets and capital balances. A factor of great importance to the firm is the cost to the firm of its existing structure.

The gearing ratio:

$$\frac{\text{Long-term debt} + \text{Preference shares}}{\text{Ordinary shareholders' funds}} \times 100$$

This ratio attempts to explain the relationship between the funds provided by the ordinary shareholders and those provided in the form of fixed and variable interest-bearing securities. Note also that, because many companies now use their bank overdraft as a long-term source of finance, it could be included in the above calculations along with the long-term debt and preference shares.

Debt/net assets ratio (US leverage)

$$\frac{\text{Long-term debt} + \text{Preference shares} + \text{Bank overdraft}}{\text{Total net assets (excluding bank overdraft from current liabilities)}} \times 100$$

Bearing in mind its limitations caused by the limitations of conventional balance sheets this shows the proportion of the net assets which are financed via fixed interest sources.

There is also Murphy Prussman gearing which was referred to earlier.

Fixed interest financing/long-term financing

$$\frac{\text{Long-term debt} + \text{Preference shares} + \text{Bank overdraft}}{\text{Total long-term financing (including bank overdraft)}} \times 100$$

This type of gearing ratio is widely used as it gives the proportion of fixed and variable interest financing to the total of the long-term financing.

The use of market values

The balance sheet ratios are book value-based and one suggested alternative designed to overcome this is to make use of market values, for example:

$$\frac{\text{Market value of long-term debt and preference shares}}{\text{Market value of ordinary shares}} \times 100$$

Market values do tend to fluctuate and so the adoption of this method is not as straight forward as it looks.

Coverage:

$$\text{Interest cover} = \frac{\text{Profit before interest and tax}}{\text{Interest (gross)}}$$

This shows the number of times the interest payable is covered by current earnings (sometimes called times interest earned).

Conclusions 努力

Management must endeavour to select forms of debt which will keep costs low and risks at a manageable level. Where a firm's gearing departs from its industry's norm could be an indication of weakness. There could, however, be quite sound reasons for such a deviation. Nowadays, gearing calculations have become more complex as a result of the uses made of bank overdrafts, hire purchase, and the hire and lease of fixed assets.

Recommended reading
Bank of England, '*Money for Business*'.
Chadwick, L. and Pike, R. *Management and Control of Capital in Industry* (CIMA).
Clarkson, G. P. E. and Elliot, B. *Managing Money and Finance* (Gower).
Paish, F. W. and Briston, R. J. *Business Finance* (Pitman).
Parker, R. H. *Understanding Company Financial Statements* (Pelican).
Weston, J. R. and Brigham, E. F. *Managerial Finance* (British Edition, Holt, Rinehart and Winston).

Dividend policy – a practical view

- '*Dividend policy is an irrelevance!*'
- '*Why pay any dividends at all?*'
- '*Directors should follow the residual theory of dividend policy.*'
- '*Dividend policy is just one big puzzle!*'

Such questions and comments are typical of those which appear from time to time in the financial press. Financial managers, accountants and academics have, in recent years, spent a great deal of time and energy debating the theoretical aspects of dividend policy. However, quite a number of the

17

theories discussed are in fact based upon assumptions which do not apply to the real world.

The purpose of this article is not the continuation of the theoretical debate relating to the dividend policy saga. The principal aim of this article is to make a realistic and practical overview of dividend policy. It must be remembered that the ultimate responsibility for dividend policy rests with the Board of Directors. Thus, from the outset, it must be noted that behavioural factors (e.g. the objectives and perceptions of each individual director) will play their part in dividend policy decision making. Human beings are very complex variables and as such are quite likely to respond differently to similar situations. If it were possible to listen in to directors discussing their proposals about dividends and dividend policy the following could be typical of the comments that may be overheard:

Director	Comment	Commentary
Les	'All we have to do is to take into account last year's dividend and this year's earnings.'	There is a lot of truth in this comment. Last year's dividend and this year's earnings are important factors which affect the dividend decision.
Dave	'I disagree, we must have stability. Even if this year's earnings are down we must maintain our dividend at its existing level.'	Many directors hold this perception, i.e. that the level of dividend should be maintained, even when earnings are falling. Market expectations could well be affected if the dividend were not maintained at last year's level. Instability could be reflected by a decrease in the share price.
Norman	'If we haven't got the cash we can't pay a dividend.'	Short, but to the point. Cash is needed to pay the dividend and ACT (Advance Corporation Tax). The payment of dividends and ACT does affect cash flow. Why go in to/increase an overdraft to pay a dividend at a time when the company needs cash?
Tom	'I've always thought that we should use the dividend to communicate our faith in the future of our company and its products.'	This is described as 'information content'. Directors do attempt to send signals to the market via their dividend policy. Market expectations do have an impact upon share prices.

Director	Comment	Commentary
Tony	'I think that we should pay little or no dividends. It appears to be bad financial management to pay out dividends and then borrow money to finance new projects. We should be ploughing back our profits, not distributing them!'	Agreed, but what reaction would be forthcoming from the market. Certain shareholders hold the shares because they provide a regular source of income in addition to capital growth. Those who advocate little or no dividends suggest that income could be generated simply by selling some of the shares.
Richard	'I agree with Tony, but we cannot ignore the "clientele effect." A lot of our shareholders, particularly the financial institutions and pension funds, have invested in us because of our high payout.'	True. Shareholders are attracted to companies with different dividend policies for a variety of reasons. Some shareholders may prefer low dividends and higher capital gains because of the effects of taxation. A dramatic change in policy could have a dramatic effect upon the share price!
Ray	'We mustn't forget that we all hold a substantial number of shares. With the current exemption limit on capital gains, I for one would prefer to see a lowering of the dividend.'	As mentioned before, directors are people and personal motives may affect their decision making. Again, it is all a question of how the market would view such a move.
Les	'We really should budget for our dividend in place of having this discussion once a year'.	Agreed. Companies ought to have a target payout and should have budgeted in their cash flow forecasts for the payment of the dividend and ACT, the ACT being due soon after the dividend has been paid.
Ray	'We must take into account any government restrictions and other constraints.'	The Board of Directors should be made aware of any government restrictions/legislation affecting distributions. Lenders may also impose restrictions on the amounts paid out as dividends. The distribution should be within the powers laid down in the company's articles of association.
Norman	'We also need to take a good look at the dividends being paid by other firms in our industry.'	If the company's dividend policy was way out of line with those of similar companies this could well have an adverse effect upon the share price.

Director	Comment	Commentary
Tom	'This company has always paid a dividend. Not to pay one now could be disastrous.'	Agreed. If the company suddenly decides not to pay a dividend the market may not approve.
Richard	Having studied the data. 'Last year's dividend was 11.5 per cent: in view of the fall in profits I propose that we pay 12 per cent for this year.'	This proposal takes into account last year's dividend, this year's earnings, stability and hopefully the availability of the cash with which to pay it.

All in favour? Yes. Carried.

Does dividend policy affect share prices?

Dividends are just one of many interacting factors which affect share prices. No doubt, dividends do influence share prices but proving it is to my mind an impossible task.

Does it make sense to pay dividends?

The answer to this question is no, it does not make sense to pay out dividends to shareholders. Many companies pay dividends and then shortly afterwards borrow more funds to finance new projects. It could be argued that to pay out a dividend is to admit defeat. The company could be construed as saying to its shareholders 'Here's your money, we're sure you can invest it elsewhere and get a better return from it than we could'. If that is the case then by all means pay a dividend. As mentioned in the commentary, shareholders do not invest in a company for the sole purpose of making a capital gain. One of their principal reasons for investing in the shares of a company is to receive an income which matches their requirements. Thus, having said no, it does not make sense to pay dividends one has to admit, taking into account the needs and expectations of the shareholders, that companies have to pay dividends.

Conclusions

Numerous factors affect the dividend and dividend policy decision and lots of questions need to be answered such as:

a) How much did we pay out last year and in earlier years?
b) Can we maintain the dividend at last year's level taking into account this year's profits?
c) Have we enough cash to pay the dividend and the associated ACT when they become due?
d) Are there any restrictions (e.g. legal, etc.) which limit the amount that can be distributed?

e) What are the expectations of our shareholders?
f) What are the expectations of the market?
g) Can we match our target payout?
h) Does a change in the environment in which the firm operates dictate a change in dividend policy?
i) What are companies in the same industrial sector doing as regards dividends?
j) Can we really use dividends to convey information to the market?
k) What do the Board of Directors consider should be done about dividends and dividend policy?

The greatest certainty about dividend policy in theory and in practice is that it will always be one big puzzle!

Further reading
Knott, G. *Understanding Financial Management* (Pan).
Pike, R. and Dobbins, R. *Investment Decisions and Financial Strategy* (Philip Allan).

The growth of the venture capital market

The 1980s have seen a dramatic increase in the number of firms participating in the venture capital market and equally as dramatic an increase in the amount of money being made available to viable business ventures. Spiro Coutarelli (1977) stated:

'. . . the European venture capital industry is very small: there are fewer than 20 institutional venture capitalists active in Europe that invest $50–75 million each year.'

Yet, by 1984, this number had risen to more than 100 (Lorenz, 1985) investing in excess of £280 m per annum (National Economic Development Office, 1986).

This article will examine this dynamic growth with particular reference to the UK, the reasons for this growth and some of the more recent developments which have been taking place.

Before commencing the study of present-day trends in venture capital it will be useful to examine, briefly, the meaning and history of venture capital.

Since the industry has developed so rapidly in recent years and now invests in a great variety of different projects, it is somewhat difficult to define accurately what is meant by the term 'venture capital'. In its broadest sense, it is merely equity finance provided to companies in the earlier stages of their development, the provider of capital being given a share in the ownership and, possibly, the management of the company. The aim of the venture capitalist, in contrast to the aims of providers of loan finance, is to make a capital gain on the investment by selling its shares at a later date when the company has achieved success and is listed on one of the share markets – the

Stock Exchange's full market or the Unlisted Securities Market – or is acquired by another company in the same industry. However, beyond this very broad definition, it becomes increasingly difficult to categorise venture capitalists. Some prefer to take minority holdings and leave the management to direct the company unhindered; others prefer to appoint non-executive board members to monitor the investment more closely; and some venture capital funds actively seek a controlling stake in the firms in order to control their investment completely. Tony Lorenz (1985) describes these as 'Hands-off', 'Reactive' and 'Hands-on' funds, respectively.

Furthermore, some funds specialise in particular industries or stages of development: some prefer high technology businesses, e.g. Advent Ltd, Rothschild's Biotechnology Investments Ltd, etc., some are regionally based, e.g. Avon Enterprise Fund PLC, London Scottish Finance Corporation Ltd., etc., and some prefer to deal with more established companies, e.g. Barclays Development Capital Ltd, Citicorp Venture Capital Ltd, etc. (Bank of England, 1985).

Providing a comprehensive, all-embracing definition of the term 'venture capital' has thus become extremely difficult and, no doubt, the term will continue to be used to cover even more forms of financial assistance as the industry develops further. Nevertheless, the origins of the modern venture capital industry can be quite clearly traced back to the MacMillan Report (1931) which first identified the 'finance gap' which existed for small firms. This report did not, however, cause a sudden rush of companies wishing to provide finance for smaller enterprises and the only surviving fund of this period is Charterhouse Development Ltd. Indeed, it was not until 1945 that the government took action to ameliorate the plight of small firms by setting up the Industrial and Commercial Finance Corporation (ICFC), now a part of Investors in Industry PLC (3i) and jointly owned by the Bank of England and the UK clearing banks. For several years, the ICFC was the dominant force in the venture capital market and it is only in recent years that it, or 3i, has had any serious competition.

The recent history of the venture capital market has shown not only a dramatic rise in the number of funds and the total amounts invested but also some very interesting developments in the types of investment being carried out. As an example, Fig. 1.3 illustrates one particular area of activity in which many venture capitalists have become involved and which was largely unheard of prior to the 1980s – *the management buy-out*. Similarly, the concept known as a 'spin-off', whereby a company sponsors certain key employees to develop a new business venture, often with the backing of a venture capitalist's finance, is comparatively new in the UK, and yet 3i have produced a marketing brochure aimed specifically at stimulating demand for this activity. Gone are the days, it would appear, when a venture capitalist bought a few shares in a company and sat back to watch the investment grow: nowadays he/she is constantly seeking to create and encourage new business activities which will require or benefit from his/her participation. Nor is it envisaged that this movement will cease in the near future – Table 3 illustrates the amazing growth in the total amounts of capital raised between 1982 and 1984:

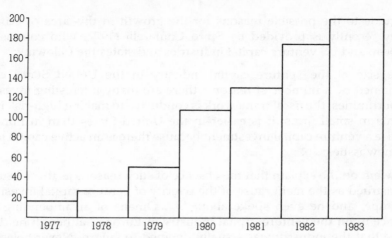

Fig. 1.3 *The growth of management buy outs: number of buy outs per year*

Source: Wright and Coyne, *Management Buy Outs*, 1985.

a growth of over 500 per cent or a compound growth rate equivalent to approximately 225 per cent! In addition, Table 3 illustrates the diminishing importance in percentage terms of the more traditional sources of finance such as the government and the banks.

Why, then, has the market for venture capital grown and developed with such a pace? Clearly the reason does not lie with government-sponsored efforts alone, although the Introduction of the Business Expansion Scheme (BES) in the UK has provided a great deal of new finance, but still less than 20 per cent of the total amount raised in 1984 (Table 3).

Table 3: Sources of capital for independent venture funds

Source	% of total capital raised		
	1982	1983	1984
Pension funds	27.4%	30.6%	40.2%
Private individuals (BES)	11.1	39.8	19.4
Insurance companies	6.9	9.2	14.7
Foreign institutions	16.6	9.0	9.8
Industrial corporations	—	—	8.6
Investment trusts	—	2.7	2.8
Banks	15.6	7.4	1.3
Government/local authorities	10.3	—	0.4
Academic institutions	4.5	—	0.2
Other	7.6	1.3	2.6
	100%	100%	100%
Total capital raised	£37.9m	£112.0m	£193.2m

Source: National Economic Development Office, *External Capital for Small Firms*, 1986.

A guide to the possible reasons for the growth in this area of economic activity recently is provided by Spiro Coutarelli (1977) who contrasts the European and US venture capital industries and states the following:

'The size of the venture capital industry in the United States can be explained by a number of reasons: there are many interesting investment opportunities; the fiscal framework is conducive to making high-risk investments in small firms; it is easier in the United States than in Europe to realise a venture capital investment because there is an active capital market for new issues; . . .'

He went on the explain that the absence of such reasons as those listed can be construed as the main cause of the paucity of venture capital investments in Europe, and he even spoke about '. . . Omens of an impending death sentence upon the venture capital industry in Europe', although he did not believe that the industry was actually doomed to failure. Nevertheless, it is clear that the environment in Europe, and particularly in the UK where the majority of funds were active, was not especially conducive to the growth and development of a strong venture capital market.

Since the early 1980s, however, much has been done to improve the situation: 1981 saw the setting up of a second market in company shares – the Unlisted Securities Market (USM) which provided a means for investors to realise their investments (that is, a new 'exit route' has been provided for venture capitalists); in 1983 the government encouraged individuals to invest in the small firms sector by allowing them tax advantages on such investments under the Business Expansion Scheme (BES); The government's Loan Guarantee Scheme has allowed many more people to raise the finance needed to start up in business and the Enterprise Allowance Scheme has encouraged even more interest and created even more opportunities for those previously unable to consider going into business for themselves. Furthermore, the government has actively encouraged the development of an 'Enterprise Culture' now being witnessed, and this encouragement continues (DTI 1988).

In addition to the above changes and developments there have been other major shifts in corporate attitudes in recent years. The 'Corporatism' of the 1960s (J. Curran, 1986) and the attitude that 'big is beautiful' have given way in the 1970s and 1980s to a view that smaller, more compact enterprises are more flexible and easy to control (P. Johnson, 1986). Thus, despite the

Table 4: Source of management buy outs

Source	No.	%
Independent company in receivership	5	4.5
Parent company in receivership	15	13.5
Parent company divesting a subsidiary	68	61.3
Previous owner on retirement	23	20.7
Total	111	100.0

Source: Wright and Coyne, *Management Buy Outs*, 1985.

'Merger Mania' concentrated on so heavily by the media, there has been a great deal of divestment taking place within companies which have sought to return to their traditional core skills (Bowater Industries, for example). The result of this move away from the large corporation has been the emergence on the market of several smaller units available for management buy-outs (see Table 4). Secondly, the general interest in assistance for small firms has focused public attention on this sector and consequently raised people's awareness about the problems and pitfalls of running or starting a new business. This change in attitude is illustrated by one of the bank managers interviewed by David Ward (Chadwick and Ward, 1982) – Bank Manager Mr B. in the article who 'held that positive involvement in businesses was essential and welcomed the movement towards equity shareholdings by the banks.'

In conclusion, the UK market place for venture capital has been greatly favoured by recent government initiatives and general trends. There are now more propositions coming forward, and as long as the percentage of these that are genuinely very viable propositions remains steady, it follows that the total number of viable propositions will increase. There are now, also, more ways in which investment monies can be repaid, either via the Unlisted Securities Market or by companies repurchasing their shares following recent legislative changes. Finally, the general climate for entrepreneurs and their financial backers has improved considerably, although some still believe more can be done to ameliorate the tax position of entrepreneurs (*The Independent*, 7 July 1988). Indeed, it is the combination of all the above factors coming together in such a short space of time (i.e. less than a decade) which has led to the impressive growth witnessed in the market for start-up and development capital. What is necessary now, it appears, is for the institutions concerned to overcome the 'bewilderment factor' (C. Woodcock, 1986) and this can only be achieved by effective marketing targetted at specific segments within the sector(s) being served. It is difficult to ascertain whether this is being performed successfully but the indications are that in the past, too much information has reached the wrong people: many commentators on venture capital (e.g. Lorenz, 1985; Coutarelli, 1977, etc.) point out that only a very small percentage of proposals (estimates given by commentators suggest 5 per cent or less) actually receive finance from venture capital institutions. To some extent, it is to be expected that in a market which experiences growth rates of the magnitude experienced in this market in recent years, information and advice on how to behave in the market may fail to keep pace with the changes taking place. After all, the professionals, of whom so much is expected, have had to familiarise themselves with an array of new products and services being offered and promoted as well as with the plethora of new firms and sources of development capital.

Bibliography

Coutarelli S. *Venture Capital in Industry* (Praeger, 1977).
Lorenz T. *Venture Capital Today* (Woodhead-Faulkner, 1985).
National Economic Development Office *Corporate Venturing*, 1987. *External Capital for Small Firms*, 1986.

Curran J. *Bolton Fifteen Years On* (The Small Business Research Trust, 1986).

Johnson P. *New Firms: an economic perspective* (Allen & Unwin, 1986).

Chadwick L. and Ward D. *Have the Banks Failed the Small Man?*, *Accountancy*, 1982.

Woodcock C. (Curran J., Stanwath J. and Watkins D., Editors) *The Survival of the Small Firm* (Gower, 1986).

The growth and development of corporate venturing

In our first article we looked at the growth of the venture capital market in the UK and Europe. In this, our second article we take a look at a relatively new UK phenomenon, corporate venturing.

Corporate venturing in the United States has been an established means of industrial co-operation and assistance to small enterprises for some years now (Coutarelli, 1977). In contrast, the United Kingdom, and indeed Europe in general, has been slow to accept and adopt this form of assistance despite the potential it holds for product generation, inter-company co-operation and financial gain for all parties involved. For this reason, there has been little attention paid to corporate venturing by most writers in the field of develop-ment finance and few companies have openly admitted their involvement in corporate venturing projects.

The principals of corporate venturing are simple: a major company takes a minority stake in a fledgling company and injects cash into that company. This may all take place with or without the participation of a third-party such as a venture capitalist (D. Oates, *Director*, June 1987). Clearly, the aim goes much further than the provision of venture capital designed to assist in the development of an enterprise and provide capital gains for the investing company (generally termed the sponsor) although, of course, this is very much a part of the project's aims. It is hoped that bringing large, well-established and well-respected corporations together with small, entrepreneurially led concerns will lead to a healthy cross-fertilisation of ideas, skills and talents to the mutual benefit of both sides; or, as the National Economic Development Office (*Corporate Venturing*, 1986) puts it:

> 'Corporate venturing offers an opportunity to combine the best of both the large and small company approaches, in order to generate opportunities for business development which might otherwise be missed.'

From the above, it is clear that the relationship that will ensue from such ventures will be far more than that of investor-investee alone. For this reason, such ventures are likely to be more successful if there is commonality between the two concerns in respect of their products, services and/or markets. This, naturally, can cause problems in that investing partners are likely to be less dispassionate than traditional venture capitalists and smaller firms are likely to fear the loss of control and possible predatory objectives from their invest-ing partner. To avoid such conflicts and doubts it can often be useful to involve venture capitalists who can mediate between the two sides, provide a buffer or an information filter to prevent one side from 'stealing' valuable technical information from the other (NEDO, 1986). Moreover, venture capitalists often lend credibility to a deal in the eyes of both parties and the outside world which may also be sceptical about the motives involved.

Having examined the practicalities and rationale behind corporate venturing, we will now go on to report some of the major findings from a research project on corporate venturing in the UK, which was carried out by The National Economic Development Office in late 1986. One thousand large companies and one thousand small companies were sent questionnaires on the topic and 335 companies replied – 107 small companies and 228 large companies. Of the small companies, only 10 of the 107 stated that they had had experience of corporate venturing whereas 76 of the 228 companies replying to the large company questionnaire claimed to have had experience of such ventures. Significantly, also, over one-third (38 of the 107 replies) of the small companies were completely ignorant of what corporate venturing actually meant.

The major benefits which were described related to greater access to information and expertise: the larger companies claimed to have been able to become involved in technologies and markets which they would not otherwise have been able to exploit; and the smaller companies which had experience of corporate venturing stressed the importance to them of the access to wider management expertise and greater credibility in the market place which the partnership afforded them. These responses were in addition to the expected benefits to the financial side of the venture.

Finally, a significant proportion (88 out of the 107 small firms and 135 of the 228 larger firms) expressed an interest in finding out more about the subject. Moreover, of the large firms which had experience of corporate venturing (76 in total) nearly one third (25) claimed it was too early to judge whether the venture had been successful, suggesting that quite a few of the ventures are comparatively recent. This would seem to confirm the conclusion drawn by the report that as a half of the 151 large firms which expressed an interest in becoming involved in such ventures in the future had not had previous experience in this field: '. . . interest in the subject is beginning to grow.' Indeed, a recent article (*The Independent*, 30 June 1988) reported that the Dutch electronics firm Philips, after several successful years of corporate venturing in the US has now decided to become involved in UK ventures.

It would, therefore, appear that there is real interest in the economy for corporate venturing projects and the benefits that can be enjoyed from them. The real question, then, is: will corporate venturing take off and succeed in the way that venture capital has? The venture capital industry was barely visible ten years ago but is now, proportionately speaking, very much as extensive as its US counterpart; whereas corporate venturing in the UK is still in its infancy and is no rival for the US market.

To attempt to answer the above question categorically at this moment in time would be unwise. Yet one can clearly identify some key areas of consideration which are crucial to the future success of British corporate venturing. Firstly, the results of the NEDO survey indicate that more must be done to introduce the subject to managers and entrepreneurs and that more education is essential. Similarly, success stories and failures must be related and discussed in order that entrepreneurs and corporate managers are fully aware of what can be involved.

Secondly, a major stumbling block in the UK, which has hindered venture capital and will hinder corporate venturing must be tackled: the obstinate proprietary attitude of entrepreneurs towards their businesses (NEDO, 1986; Lorenz, 1985). It is still true today that many owners are extremely reluctant to relinquish total ownership of their enterprises to any outside party. Venture capitalists have repeatedly complained of this stubborn British attitude and if entrepreneurs are unwilling to allow a comparatively passive third-party to enjoy a percentage share of the business, it is highly unlikely that they will allow such ownership to pass into the hands of companies whom they have even greater reason to mistrust – either because of suspicions as to predatory motives or due to the fact that they may be, or become, potential rivals. This attitude may have changed slightly following the introduction of new capital markets – the USM and Over-the-Counter Market – but the NEDO, in 1986, still recognised that: 'Of the 12 small company respondents who had considered but rejected the option of corporate venturing, eight mentioned the potential loss of control, independence or identity and five the fear of restrictions or interference.' This would seem to confirm the perception that the proprietors of small firms in the UK continue to place a high value on ownership and control at the expense of other objectives. This attitude is in marked contrast to the approach of entrepreneurs in the USA who put greater emphasis on profit, are much less interested in retaining complete control of their businesses and are less worried about interference.

The report does suggest that to protect the interests of both sides in a corporate venturing proposal a document be drawn up to ensure confidentiality and autonomy, and it seems reasonable to suppose that this document could be extended to guard against the problems of interference. Certainly having a venture capital fund as a third-party may help in such situations, but ultimately some greater degree of trust and understanding needs to be built up. To facilitate this it would appear to be sensible to involve larger groups, such as the CBI, who could draw up guidelines and even police corporate venturing to ensure that fair play is upheld.

Finally, a possible hurdle which was mentioned by a local director of a 3i regional office concerns the attitude of the larger enterprises towards corporate venturing. There appears to be a sentiment amongst industrialists that any product or service worth supporting must be worthwhile enough to pursue and hence they would wish to have 100 per cent control of the relevant product or service. This would seem to contradict the view that corporate bodies are seeking to concentrate more on their core skills and are more willing to buy in peripheral services in the modern climate (NEDO, 1986), and instead suggests that good ideas are less likely to be supported outside the business and more likely to be kept for in-house development. If this is true then corporate venturing is doomed to failure; but if it is only true of the more medium-sized businesses then attitudes may change in the light of the experiences of those who actively participate in corporate venturing.

Success, therefore, is not guaranteed for corporate venturing and some obstacles will need to be overcome, but the possibilities are exciting and rewarding if greater interest, wider participation and a more co-ordinated approach can be created.

Bibliography

Coutarelli, S. *Venture Capital in Europe* (Praeger, 1977).

Lorenz, T. *Venture Capital Today* (Woodhead-Faulkner, 1985).

National Economic Development Office *Corporate Venturing*, 1987.

National Economic Development Office *External Capital for Small Firms*, 1986.

Oates, D. 'Corporate Venturing: Big Help for Small Firms', *The Director*, June 1987.

Wright, M. and Coyne, J. *Management Buy-outs* (Croom-Helm, 1985).

Woodcock, C., Chapter 3 of Curran, J., Stanworth, J., and Watkins, D., (eds) *The Survival of the Small Firm* Vol. I (Gower, 1986).

2

The financing of the small business sector

The first of the readings looks at the problems facing small firms. It reviews the literature covering reports up to and including the progress report published by the Wilson Committee in 1977. It concludes that one of the major problems facing small firms is a 'communication gap'. Although this article was published some time ago, it was included because of its interesting historical content and also because, in the author's opinion, even today it would appear that there is still a 'communication gap' between the providers of finance and those who seek it.

The second reading in this chapter examines the relationship and services provided by firms of accountants to their small business clients. It suggests that many more firms of accountants could provide book-keeping services and, in doing so, carry out a continuous audit and be in a position to provide more relevant information for their small business clients. By helping their small business clients they are, in fact, helping themselves.

Three of the readings take a look at the role of banks and in particular the attitudes of bank managers. As a mini-piece of research, the findings were quite revealing and very interesting indeed. Although a lot of water has passed under the bridge since these articles were written and the banks now take great pains in targeting the small business community, much of what was said still applies today, e.g. bankers still like to have some security for an advance.

The problems of financing small and medium-sized firms

Small businesses have been likened to the flowers in the spring: rich in diversity, often colourful, full of the promise of better things to come. The sturdy blossom into full maturity, the weaker disappear to be replaced by a joyous new crop the following year. A decade ago, such a lyrical view might have passed unchallenged. Today, as the seeds of enterprise are withering on increasingly stony ground, romanticising about small businesses is as damaging as it is misleading.[1]

The fact is that, over the last two decades, the small business sector has been in consistent decline. This is not a uniquely British phenomenon: the same has been happening in Germany, France, Japan and North America. But whereas overseas the trend has now largely been arrested, in Britain the casualty rate has increased.[1]

Various studies of the problems of small firms in different countries have shown that one of the most common features is the complaint by entrepreneurs about the difficulty in financing the business.[2]

In 1931 the Macmillan Report was published, and this highlighted the great difficulties experienced by smaller companies when attempting to raise longer-term finance in relatively small amounts. Macmillan believed this to be mainly the result of a gap in the supply of suitable funds to support the growth of smaller companies.[3] This phenomenon became known as the 'Macmillan Gap', which has been described as 'the lack of provision for small and medium-sized firms of long-term capital in amounts too small for public issues'.[4] It led to the setting-up of various institutions specialising in the financing of small firms, notably Charterhouse Industrial Development, Credit for Industry, and Leadenhall Securities. But these institutions could tackle only part of the problem. Accordingly, in 1945, the major clearing banks, with support from the Bank of England, set up the Industrial and Commercial Finance Corporation (ICFC), which at once became and remains by far the most important institutional provider of long-term capital to small and medium enterprises in Britain.

It has been argued that it is a misuse of scarce resources to provide finance for inefficient small businesses, and that the existence of the Macmillan Gap is a good thing. The existence of the gap helps to ensure that the less efficient firms in the economy are squeezed out, or at least not encouraged to grow,[5] thus directing finance to the more efficient firms in order to promote their growth.

However, it was stated in the Radcliffe Report of 1959 that 'it is of great importance to our competitive position that we should not lose the fruit of our ideas and inventions to our international competitors, and that firms in this country should not be prevented by lack of funds, or by ignorance of the sources of capital open to them, from putting them to use.'[6] One of its principal findings was that the existing institutions of the day, with some modifications, were probably adequate to meet the needs of the smaller firms, but that the growth of these firms could be seriously impeded because they lack some of the facilities open to larger companies for obtaining finance. The report also pointed out that it would be highly beneficial for the smaller firms to acquire a better knowledge of the various financial institutions. Thus the report contained three specific recommendations for the improvement of facilities available to the small firm:

a) that joint stock banks be ready to offer term loan facilities, as an alternative to a running overdraft, for creditworthy industrial and commercial customers;
b) that the upper limit on the size of transactions in which the ICFC were

permitted to engage should be reviewed in the light of the change in the value of money; and

c) the creation of a corporation to facilitate the commercial exploitation of technical innovation.

Each of the above recommendations has been implemented in some form, term loans are now provided by the clearing banks (credit policy permitting), either directly or through their subsidiary and associated companies. There is now no formal upper limit on the size of ICFC's investments. The technological gap has been met, at least in part, by the creation of new institutions such as Technical Development Capital Ltd (TDC), now an ICFC subsidiary.

Since 1959 there has been a remarkable expansion in the number of bodies providing finance and in the services offered. The willingness of these institutions to cater for small and medium-sized firms is attested by the appearance of a number of venture capital companies, also by the expansion of London merchant banks into the provinces, by the development of local merchant banks or issuing houses in most major cities, and by the entry of the clearing banks into new types of business.

The Bolton Report

In Britain the Bolton Report, published in 1971, is the authoritative source of information on small firms. The definition of a small firm as given by the Bolton Report, is in general terms one employing less than 200 people, although there are various qualifications. In the retailing sector, for example, a turnover of £50 000 or less (1971 figures) is the criterion; in the wholesale trades, a turnover of £200 000 or less; in the construction industry, up to 25 employees; in road transport, five vehicles or less. Perhaps more important than the statistical limitations, some of which, like turnover, have been taken over by inflation, are the three characteristics that Bolton sees as typical of a small firm. A small business is one that is managed by its owners or part-owners in a personalised way. It has a relatively small market, and it is independent, in that it does not form part of a larger enterprise and its own owner-managers are free from outside control in taking their principal decisions.[4] On the subject of finance, the Bolton Report said that small firms suffer a number of genuine disabilities, by comparison with larger firms, in seeking finance from *external* sources:

a) The periodic 'squeezes' and official ceilings on bank lending tend to hit small firms harder than large firms;

b) That small firms have great difficulty in raising medium-term finance in relatively small amounts (i.e. between £5000 and £50 000), and, to this extent, the 'Macmillan Gap' was still in existence;

c) Some institutional facilities (e.g. the Stock Exchange) available to large firms are not available to small firms. (New issue market is still effectively closed to firms wishing to raise less than £250 000 in equity or a much larger figure in loan capital);[7]

d) Small borrowers must generally pay higher rates of interest than large borrowers;[8]
e) Many small firms lack knowledge about sources of finance. One of the Research Reports commissioned[9] found that, in manufacturing industry, no less than 92 per cent of respondents had not been involved in any attempt to obtain finance through financial institutions other than their local commercial bank. The reasons for this being ignorance, prejudice and moral scruples or simply because the firms concerned did not need additional finance or were not sufficiently credit-worthy. Another report high-lighted the inadequacy and fragmented nature of the advice and information available to small firms on financial and related matters;[10] and
f) Thus, many small firms are prejudiced against borrowing. In this respect the psychological attitude of small businesses is an important factor. It has been shown quite clearly that a vast number of small businesses simply dislike and mistrust institutions (private or public) on the grounds that they threaten their independence.[11]

However, the Bolton Report said that most of these disabilities reflect the higher cost of lending in small amounts or the higher risk of lending to small borrowers. Therefore, it did not recommend the creation of a new institution for the provision of finance to small firms, nor did it support the provision of finance at subsidised rates. It did, however, recommend the setting-up of a central Small Firms Information Service to help to bridge the 'information gap'. This service would have two broad functions:

a) The education of managers of small firms in techniques for evaluating their development proposals and the presentation of these to financial institutions; and in such matters as keeping up-to-date financial records and making cash flow projections without which potential lenders are discouraged.
b) The collection and dissemination of information about the available sources of finance and the extent of its supply, and, in particular, improving the knowledge of accountants and solicitors in these matters so that they may be able to give better advice to help small businesses cope with their increasingly complex environment.

It has, however, been argued[12] that accountants from whom advice is frequently sought are either incapable of giving the advice, or do not give impartial advice. Most accountants tend to restrict their advice by introducing one group of their clients who need finance to another group who are likely to provide it.

The Bolton Report stated that, of the 800 000 small firms in the UK, only one-third look for external finance, the majority tend to finance their growth from retained profits. It was also observed that many firms do not even take the most elementary steps to help themselves, such as contacting their local Chamber of Commerce, Trade Association or any private (e.g. CBI) or public (e.g. Department of Trade and Industry) national body. Thus, it was concluded that, on the supply side, the Macmillan Gap had been filled by the development of institutions such as ICFC, Charterhouse and others, and that as it now stands there is no imperfection in supply. Whereas, on the demand side, there existed an 'information gap' as a result of lack of knowledge, prejudice and the fragmented nature of advice and information available.

The Government announced acceptance of the Bolton Report's recommendations for the formation of a Small Firms Advisory Bureau on 19 August 1971. Since that date, the Department of Industry has set up Small Firms Information Centres in certain principal industrial centres.

For current publications contact your local **Small Firms Information Service.**

Since their introduction the Centres appear to have been quite active and have certainly contributed towards the closing of the information gap. They have even introduced a 'dial-an-answer' service using their nationwide network of regional enquiry centres.

Mr J. E. Bolton, Chairman of the Committee of Inquiry on Small Firms (the Bolton Report), commented in May 1976 on what had been happening during the five years since the publication of his Committee's report on the small firms' business sector. He said that, despite the implementation of most of the 60 or more recommendations in the 1971 report, small firms were generally worse off and had suffered more than large companies.[13] He blamed the economic climate in which they are operating, with its high rate of inflation causing severe cash shortage, higher taxation and the increased burden of legislation, combined with poor trading conditions, for this state of affairs.

The original report found that over 90 per cent of outside finance used by small firms came from their local banks. Thus, according to Mr Bolton, some form of priority should be given to the small firms' sector and some way found to increase the discretionary lending limits of local managers, which had not kept up with inflation over the five years in question.

He also believed that the combined effects of capital gains tax and capital transfer tax could emasculate our most successful small and medium-sized companies within a generation. Thus, he cited the principal problems of small firms as follows:

a) Their major problem is still the availability of working capital, and this rests fairly and squarely with the clearing banks. The double squeeze of high inflation – causing a need for increased working capital just to stand still – and depreciation in the value of the assets which the small firm can offer as security has caused an ever-increasing gap.

b) Although, in response to the Bolton Report, the Government have made a number of useful concessions, the crushing burden of taxation continues to be a critical problem.

c) Excessive paperwork caused by legislation and administrative requirements of Government Departments is another big worry. The original report estimated a statistical load on the small firm to be about four times the size of that of large firms. Of the 15 recommendations made, most were actioned, but the tide has flooded back, VAT being a major culprit.

34

d) The volume of Government legislation is an area of great concern. The baby of enterprise is surely being thrown out with the bathwater in seeking to ensure uniformity of action regardless of the cost.

What ought to be done?

Much can be done to reverse the above problems. Greater authority must be given to the local bank manager who alone can assess the real security behind increased current assets on a going concern basis, future cash flow and – the absolute essential – the skill of the people running the small business.

As a minimum, our inheritance taxes should be no more damaging to private business than those existing for our competitors in Germany, France 血緣. and Holland, where consanguinity rules are very favourable to business 親族. assets passed down to 'the family'. A further step could be to reduce capital gains tax on the transfer of business assets, say, by 1 per cent per annum, so that someone transferring a business built up by him over a 30-year period would be liable to little or no capital gains tax. Another area which receives little publicity is taxation on new businesses. If they are unincorporated, the first year can be used as the basis for the first three years' assessments, which is not so if a limited company is formed. Also, the fact that tax losses cannot be set-off against other taxation unless the loss-making company happens to be part of a larger group. All these contribute towards a disincentive for private individuals to risk their savings in backing an entrepreneur.

So, just what can the small firm possibly do to stay afloat? In Chapter 10 of the Bolton Report eight areas were listed in which it was generally considered that small businessmen could usefully improve their performance, and hence profitability. They were: finance, costing and control information, organising routines, marketing, information use and retrieval, personnel management, technological change and production scheduling/purchase controls. These suggestions remain just as valid today – in fact, they are even more valid because the total climate of operation for small firms has become even more difficult.[13]

What is being done?

In December 1977 the 'Wilson Committee',[14] headed by Sir Harold Wilson, published a progress report reviewing a multitude of points and proposals relating to the financing of small firms. This report did not contain any firm conclusions or recommendations. However, it did stress that various proposals for reducing the burden of taxation had been vigorously emphasised by those responsible for providing it with information. Many of the other points put to the Committee confirm the findings of earlier reports and are in agreement with the numerous articles published in professional journals and the financial press, e.g. the decline of the personal investor in companies; that equity capital is more expensive for smaller companies; the burden placed upon small firms resulting from increased legislation and statistical requirements; and the existence of an 'information gap'.

佳辰 The progress report also lists various proposals[15] put forward for the assistance of small firms which include:

a) Government backing and support to finance increases in the level of finished stock; provide an 'innovation insurance corporation' to guarantee finance for new ventures; finance leasing by small companies and consultancy expenditure;
b) An Export Credits Guarantee Department-type facility to underwrite technical risk, and the underwriting of, say, 80 per cent of additional funds required to finance the entry into a new export market;
c) A 'high-risk lending support fund' financed by a levy on overdraft lending;
d) Changes in company legislation; and
e) An information office to bring together new technology-based firms and appropriate sources of finance.

'The most useful thing the Government can do for the small business is to reduce the burden of taxation,' was the message from the accountancy bodies to Harold Lever.[16] This adds further support for the views expressed to the Wilson Committee. The CCAB also stated that they consider that the most serious problem facing small companies is still the difficulty of obtaining adequate finance at reasonable prices.

Does the information gap still exist?

If and when reliable information is available for small and medium-sized businesses, another major problem will be that of ensuring that it reaches the correct destination, i.e. where it can be most useful.

It is argued that much of the publicity material of financial institutions is far too general to be of use to smaller companies.[17] What it ignores is the task of educating the small business into exactly what is required when submitting an application for funds. It is also apparent that even the knowledge and services provided by accountants do not reach a significant section of the business community.[18]

Since the publication of the Bolton Report in 1971, information relating to the finance of small companies has grown in quantity and quality and is not now in short supply (e.g. information provided by the Small Firms Information Service, Trade Associations, ICFC, banks, etc.). The only problem is, as stated earlier, that of making sure appropriate information reaches the right quarters, thus avoiding a *communication* gap. Weaknesses in this area are the result of a possible reluctance or inability of local bank managers and professional advisers to recommend other sources of finance.[7]

Summary

The main conclusion of the Bolton report was that the Macmillan Gap relating to the provision of finance to small and medium-sized firms no longer exists.

It was apparent, however, that what did exist was an 'information gap' which can work both ways. One of its principal recommendations, the setting-up of a central bureau for, amongst other things, the collection and dissemination of information, has been implemented. Thus, regional Small Firms Information Centres, together with various other public and private institutions, generate between them sufficient information which now ensures that there is no shortage in the availability of information. The main problem is to ensure that relevant information reaches the user, as a great amount of information never reaches those for whom it was intended.

Writing some five years after the Bolton Report, Mr J. E. Bolton considers, despite the implementation of most of the sixty or more recommendations, that small firms are now even worse off as a result of inflation, higher taxation, the increased burden of Government legislation and the shortage of working capital.

The progress report published by the Wilson Committee in December 1977 contained numerous points and proposals put to the Committee which were in agreement with those expressed by Bolton,[13] CCAB and others. However, words are not enough, what is really required is some positive *action*.

References
[1]Brown, Rosemary 'Why Small Business Matters', *Management Today* December 1976.
[2]Wood, E. G. *Financial Aid to Small and Medium Enterprises* A Paper presented at the European and International Congress on Small and Medium Enterprises. Brussels, September 1976.
[3]Macmillan Report 1931.
[4]Bolton Report of the Committee of Inquiry on Small Firms. HMSO, November 1971.
[5]Bates, J. *The Financing of Small Business* (Sweet and Maxwell, 1969).
[6]Radcliffe Report 1959.
[7]Smith, B. D. *Financing Problems of Small Growth Companies* MBA Dissertation, Bradford University, 1977.
[8]Tamari, M. Research Report No. 16, *A Postal Questionnaire Survey of Small Firms: An Analysis of Financial Data* Committee of Inquiry on Small Firms, HMSO 1972.
[9]Merret Cyriax Associates. Research Report No. 12, *Dynamics of Small Firms* Committee of Inquiry on Small Firms, HMSO 1972.
[10]Economists Advisory Group. Research Report No. 4. *Financing Facilities for Small Firms.* Committee of Inquiry on Small Firms, HMSO 1971.
[11]Golby, C. W. and Johns, G. Research Report No. 7, *Attitude and Motivation* Committee of Inquiry on Small Firms, HMSO 1971.
[12]Economists Advisory Groups. Research Report No. 5. *Problems of the Small Firms in Raising External Finance. The results of a Sample Survey.* Committee of Inquiry on Small Firms, HMSO 1971.
[13]Bolton, J. E. 'Keeping Small Firms Afloat', *Management Accounting* May 1976.
[14]Progress Report, Committee to Review the Functioning of Financial Institutions, 15 December, 1977.
[15]Reid, Margaret. 'Let Tax Concessions Help Small Man'. *Financial Times*, 16 December 1977.

[16]'Reduce Tax Burden To Help Small Companies', *Accountancy Age*, 6 January 1978.

[17]Strong, R. M. 'Finance for the Smaller Company', *Management Consultant*, June 1974.

[18]Hartiagn, P. 'Why Companies Fail', *Certified Accountant*, December 1976.

Towards a better service for the small business

How often have you heard one of your colleagues protest in anger that 'this chap is an imbecile' or words to that effect? What they really mean is that the accounting records of the particular client are very poor indeed and/or obtaining information from him is rather like trying to get blood out of a stone.

An important factor apparently overlooked by numerous accountants is that their small clients are not bookkeepers, do not want to become bookkeepers, and neither have the time nor the inclination to keep satisfactory books of account. The small clients to which I refer are the numerous sole traders and partnerships encountered by the majority of practices and are much smaller than the various limits included in the definition of a small firm in the Bolton Report of 1971.

In the first quarter of this year, I carried out a survey into the volume of bookkeeping and computer services undertaken by accountants in public practice for their small clients, using a sample of 35 practices in the West Riding of Yorkshire. The results are shown in Table 5.

Table 5: Volume of bookkeeping services currently undertaken by accountants for small clients

% Level of service provided	Percentage of practices
For less than 5% of small clients	83
For 5% up to 10% of small clients	11
For over 10% of small clients	6
	100

Many of the accountancy firms contacted were careful to point out that they would, in fact, be prepared to provide a bookkeeping service for their small clients if they were requested to do so. A bookkeeping service has been taken to mean writing up the books from original data and preparing VAT returns and not, as in many cases, simply writing up the nominal ledger. The vast majority of firms agreed that the principal reason for such a low level of bookkeeping service was simply one of *cost to the client*. Other explanations put forward were:

a) The introduction of VAT had forced many small clients into improving their recording systems.

b) 'We are accountants, not bookkeepers.' Practices past and present have encouraged small clients to keep their own books and, as a result, a considerable proportion of small clients were already adequately served.
c) Quite a number of firms stressed that they prefer to educate their clients into keeping satisfactory records.
d) To provide such a service for small clients is commercially not viable.
e) The use of pre-printed books by small clients, e.g., analysed cash books and VAT books, some of which are stocked and recommended by the accountancy firms. The manufacturers of these pre-printed bookkeeping systems have certainly been able to cash in on the bookkeeping service gap, but this is another story.

The proportion of practices which had circularised clients in the past, or were now actively engaged in encouraging small clients to make greater use of such a service, amounted to only 17 per cent. A mere 6 per cent of firms consulted admitted to using the services of a computer for recording and preparation of accounts and returns for their small clients. Just a few years ago, this percentage would have been nil.

Assessing the benefits – saving time

The benefits of providing a bookkeeping service for small clients are several and most important of all is that the provision of a bookkeeping service should bring about savings in the time taken to complete the various returns, final audit, preparation of accounts and agreement of tax liability. Thus, the cost to the clients of this service should be offset by savings arising from a reduction in audit and accountancy fees payable. As one accountant commented: 'If I did not keep my clients' books and prepare their VAT Returns it would probably cost them far more if I had to sort out the mess caused by do-it-yourself bookkeeping'.

Earlier preparation of accounts and returns means earlier billing of clients and earlier cash inflows. It should also mean that the clients' records and returns (e.g. VAT returns) are more accurate and kept up to date. This should enable practices to carry out some form of continuous audit (e.g. vouching throughout the year/preparation of various schedules), which in turn would no doubt ensure that seasonal peaks in the work-flow are minimised.

The partners of accountancy firms should, therefore, be in a better position to plan work-flow and budget the time and resources necessary to service their small client population. With this in mind, it would be quite useful to keep a budget and actual comparative record for each client.

Analysis of the budget

This analysis of the budget and actual comparative time records should provide the answers to a multitude of questions, including:

a) When are bookkeepers required?

b) How many bookkeepers must be employed?
c) Does the practice need to engage any part-time staff?
d) How much should clients have to pay for the bookkeeping service?

The information generated by the analysis would, in addition to assisting practices to budget time and resources more effectively, also act as a valuable aid towards improving the quality control of their professional services. The books could be written-up on a monthly basis and, as a result, earlier discovery of errors, fraud and inadequacies in the client's recording system is far more likely. Early detection means that early corrective action can be taken to remedy the situation. This regular writing up of the accounting records should also ensure that the client is informed of the likelihood of a possible liquidation, i.e. it provides an early warning system.

A closer watch can be kept on the small client population to ensure that information is available when required, e.g. to fulfil the demands frequently imposed upon the small business sector by new legislation.

The policy change introduced by the Inland Revenue in 1977 relating to the examination of business accounts is yet another indication of the necessity to maintain satisfactory accounting records. The new approach means that the Revenue will devote a vast proportion of its time and effort on those accounts which, in the opinion of the District Inspector, warrant an in-depth investigation into the records and vouchers from which they were prepared. Thus, where small clients do have accurate and up-to-date records kept by their accountants, they have nothing to fear and should be liable to far less interference from the Revenue.

The bookkeeping systems could be designed to meet the needs of each individual small business. In fact, it ought to be possible to adopt a standard system, suitably amended, to allow for variations between client firms. This usage of standard systems should lead to savings in clerical effort and ensure that information which should be produced is readily available, accurate and not hidden among a mass of meaningless data. In reply to the comment, 'many of our clients are already adequately served on the bookkeeping side', one is forced to ask the question, 'but are they in fact adequately served?'

The truth is that some will have quite sound bookkeeping systems, but a large proportion, whether written up by the client or others, fall far short of providing accountancy firms with a suitable foundation from which to prepare accurate accounts and computations. The practices therefore have to carry out a considerable amount of additional work simply to convert the accounting records written up by clients into a meaningful set of figures. This means the client has the inconvenience of having to provide a constant flow of further information and also increases the time charge. Thus, the cost to the client is greater than if proper records had been maintained.

An attractive proposition

It would be possible to employ both full-time and part-time bookkeeping staff, some of whom could work at home, e.g. married women, retired former employees. This could be quite an attractive proposition. Besides providing the practice with some flexibility to expand or contract as demands on the service fluctuate, there should also be significant savings in such overheads as light and heat, office space, etc.

It has been argued by R. D. Back, of the Department of Commerce, James Cash University of North Queensland, in 'Accountants advising the small firms' (*Accountancy*, October 1977) that accountants should be encouraged to do less handwritten bookkeeping and spend more time advising their clients. However, if they are to fulfil this important role, the provision of more accurate and up-to-date information on which to base decisions is essential. The practices would be in frequent contact with their small clients and would, therefore, be in a far better position to advise them. The advice would be based upon the information prepared by the practices themselves.

Better communication

Another benefit resulting from the frequency of the periodic contact with the client, also relating to the accountant's role as adviser, is the possibility of closing the 'communication gap'. There is an abundance of information intended for small firms, e.g. sources of finance, much of which never reaches them, hence the 'communication gap'. The professional practices are therefore in an ideal position to 'bridge that gap' and direct relevant information towards their small clients, e.g. services of small business centres and ICFC, etc.

A good alternative to handwritten bookkeeping systems for small clients, adopted by only two out of the 35 practices consulted, is to engage the services of a computer bureau. This involves educating the client at the outset on how to complete a small number of input documents, and the rest is pretty straightforward.

The input forms (forms used in a receipts and payments system developed to deal with incomplete records) when completed by the client consist of: bank payment form; cash payments form; money received sheet and bank lodgements. All the client has to do is list the transactions giving information such as payee, invoice number, gross amount, VAT code, account code number, narrative (certain account codes must be accompanied by narrative). The accountants complete two principal input documents: the journal entries sheet, for opening entries, depreciation, stocks, etc., and the reversible journal entries sheet, for accrued and prepaid items, etc.

The original input data is checked, punched and verified before processing, the result being the creation of a sound data base providing a wide range of information. The computer can supply print-outs of accounts (monthly, quarterly, yearly, etc.), VAT return details; tax computation; control accounts and departmental accounts. The system also ensures that there is a satisfactory audit trail. The cost of the system is not nearly as much as one might envisage.

Could the Institute's paper on Professional Independence be interpreted using the words of one of the accountants contacted, to mean, 'Thou shalt not write up thy client's books?' One would think not. However, the statement

41

does point out that where accountants do prepare accounting records it is difficult to draw the line between appropriate and inappropriate involvement. The risk of impairing professional independence must therefore never be overlooked.

In response to the ethics discussion paper the Labour Economics Finance and Taxation Association has called for a ban on auditors carrying out additional work for clients. Where accountants do offer a bookkeeping and/or computer service for small clients this should in no way restrict their professional independence. The provision of accurate and up-to-date records is a most admirable aim, worth striving for, quite ethical and an aid to objectivity.

Accountancy firms should provide their small clients with a more sympathetic and comprehensive bookkeeping service to meet their particular needs. The cost-to-client barrier need not be as great as envisaged by the majority of practitioners consulted, as this should be offset by savings in audit and accountancy charges. The research indicates that there is scope for great expansion in the areas considered and that, in recent years, there have been signs of an awakening within the profession. Offering the small client a bookkeeping service and utilising the services provided by a computer bureau are both worthy of serious consideration. Remember, the small firms of today may be the large firms of tomorrow.

Have the banks failed the small man?

'Every banker that we visited was only willing to lend against last year's balance sheet, not next year's cash flow' . . . 'The banks don't really understand the needs of the small business' . . . 'The personal guarantee is the anathema that ends conversations with banks' . . .

A barrage of such criticism has been aimed at the banks, and no doubt we shall go on hearing it for some time. Does it stem from a small minority of disgruntled would be entrepreneurs? Have the banks failed in this area?

A less often asked question, and perhaps a more appropriate one, is: 'how do the bank managers themselves feel about small businesses?'

To find out, five managers were asked for their honest and strictly personal views. The interviews were carefully conducted and structured in such a way as to obtain an objective observer's picture rather than the banks' 'official view'.

Interview 1

Mr A, a Northerner, aged about 55, was grey-haired, friendly-faced and, one felt, immediately trustworthy. Clearly here was a man from whom you would buy a second-hand car with full confidence.

He agreed that bankers have a tendency to be conservative and cautious by nature, but hinted that it may possibly be different further south.

On the subject of the provision of security, he was quite emphatic, describing it as 'essential' for new ventures because he believed it revealed the necessary commitment and provided an incentive to the entrepreneur. Asked about entrepreneurs, he was equally unequivocal and saw their main problem as being a lack of professionalism.

He criticised those businesses not employing an accountant, and criticised the accountants that were employed!

'Schemes are not thought through properly – they are aware of how much they need now, but have no idea about requirements in one year's time.'

The lack of planning by many entrepreneurs clearly added to Mr A's concern about adequate security, and he stated that he always had to be aware of the possibility of failure, and consequently was also very much concerned with break-up value.

'What they don't realise is that it is not our money.'

He believed that term loans were now adequately covered. Was this something he now dealt with on a regular basis? 'Well not regularly – banks aren't really supposed to borrow short and lend long, you know.'

To increase the size of the small business sector, two things must happen; either the birth rate must rise or the death rate must decline. How, for instance, could Mr A's bank help to reduce the death rate of small firms? Should his bank be more involved in businesses through equity holdings and the provision of management consultancy skills?

Mr A was adamant. On equity: 'It's not our job'. And the actual performance of small firms: 'It's the responsibility of the directors of the firm.'

Mr A created a clear impression, endorsed by his comment – 'My responsibilities are to my depositors and shareholders' – which seemed eminently sensible and unarguably true.

Could it be that critics were correct in their analysis of what the banks were not doing, but wrong to assert that it was the responsibility of banks to do those things in the first place?

Interview 2

Mr B, aged 36, was obviously different from Mr A in both professional and personal outlook. He stressed that there was very little to choose between the main banks in terms of facilities and schemes, and that the main difference was not between Lloyds and Barclays or the National Westminster and the Midland Bank *but between the individual managers*.

An intriguing point of view; for if the lending policies pursued by banks depended on the temperament of the management, entrepreneurs would be well advised to 'shop around', and it should not be assumed that because one particular Midland Bank manager had refused to grant a loan, the next Midland Bank manager would do the same.

Mr B discounted the theory of differences in temperament on a geographical basis, but did believe that age may be an important factor. He felt that the 'new breed' of managers were now subjected to a programme of training far more complex and diverse than was the case even 10 years ago.

His views on the banks' role in aiding small businesses would find much favour with critics. He firmly held that positive involvement in businesses was essential and welcomed the movement towards equity shareholding by the banks. The question of security was the last consideration on his mind when appraising a loan application. But security did reveal a commitment by the entrepreneur and a willingness to share the risk. As Mr B put it: 'Security isn't the prime consideration but I may be slightly anxious about an entrepreneur who is reluctant to put up security.'

He shared Mr A's views on the poor performance of accountants and blamed many failures on them for not introducing effective control procedures.

From his own experience, he was satisfied that his bank was doing all that could be asked of it, and his personal belief was that the real problems facing small businesses had more to do with bureaucratic controls, regulations and taxation.

Mr B was clearly the type of manager of whom the banks' critics would approve, but it is interesting to note that he did not see himself as being 'typical'.

Interview 3

When telephoned, Mr C promised to reveal the practicalities of banking, as opposed to the academic view. 'Come and see me and I'll tell you the way it really is!'

He was forthright and very critical. 'The Regional Head Office often rejects the projects I submit, but it doesn't know the customer as I do – the people over there may not want to make a mistake when they are moving on in a year or two.'

Evidently Mr C was not a happy man! He was extremely perturbed at the interpersonal and organisational problems associated with a large organisation. However, he did express a deep concern for the small firms' sector, and strongly believed that the clearing banks were the only organisations capable of doing something to help – but he also believed that at present they were not ready and indeed would to some extent always be hampered by an inbuilt aversion to risk situations.

He did detect the gradual emergence of more liberal attitudes, but as he put it, when referring to older managers: 'You can't change the habits of 30 years overnight.'

He was convinced that the Government Loan Guarantee Scheme was 'just what was needed' to counteract the conservatism of certain managers.

A notable difference between Mr C and the previous interviewees was the pressure he appeared to be under. He revealed a frustration at the amount of trivia he had to deal with, and the fact that this diverted him from more important tasks.

'You hear all about these wonderful schemes, but there are just too many to be able to know them in any detail . . . I'm encouraged (from above) to go out and visit places and to sit down with clients and give help, but it's often just a case of handing them a leaflet . . . Loan appraisals are hard work – if I'm having a bad day or I have too much work I'm inclined to say "No".'

Mr C believed that the banks were misleading people – and possibly themselves – into believing that they were now specialists in all areas when, in fact, he saw himself in danger of becoming a 'Jack of all trades' and very definitely master of none!

Questioned about equity holdings he admitted that he had had no involvement 'but I have heard it happens'.

He was, however, optimistic that changes in attitudes and organisational restructures would occur. 'The people at the top – and I mean in London – are very determined, but we are a large organisation, and change takes time.'

Interview 4

Mr D was in sympathy with Mr C: 'We too get thousands of new things passed down to us, and quite often I only have time for a cursory glance – I can't possibly deal with them all.'

He also endorsed Mr C's views on a manager now becoming a 'Jack of all trades', and pointed out his master file, over four inches thick, containing short descriptions of his own bank's services. 'Little did I know, when I entered banking, that I would have to become an insurance agent, a computer manager, a travel agent and so forth.'

'Without a personal knowledge of customers,' he added, 'how could ventures be confidentially undertaken without security?'

Did he then feel that the banks were not the right institutions to deal with venture capital? He emphatically denied this. His bank did in fact have a subsidiary that dealt with new start-up situations and which was prepared to take equity shares. He could not quite remember the name of the subsidiary, but stressed that it did exist.

Mr D's bank had a well-publicised advisory service which, according to the bank's publications provided specialists in almost all fields. He believed that this service was as good as it professed to be, but regrettably he didn't 'know much about that side of things'.

Following up earlier comments about the changes in the banking sector, he agreed that a definite change could be detected. 'The attitude now is that if a bank manager doesn't, occasionally, back a loser, he can't possibly be operating in the right areas. In my own case, I tend to regard it as my money, and I don't like to lose it.'

Asked what he, as a banker, could do to help small firms he said: 'I think we already do enough, and anyway do we really want more small businesses? After all, if a small business starts up, he must be taking business away from someone else.'

Mr D was clearly satisfied with the performance of his own bank. While we may have inferred that he was not wholly in touch with all the developments introduced by his bank to meet the requirements of small firms, it would be wrong to assume that this dramatically impaired his performance. Even if he was not fully aware of the actual details of the various schemes (and this looked more and more like a hopeless task), he did seem to be the kind of manager that would quickly recognise his own weaknesses in a given situation and refer the entrepreneur to people with more experience.

One thing that did emerge was the conflict resulting from the downward pressure caused by top-level determination to become less security conscious and, at the grass-roots level, the obligations felt by managers to shareholders and depositors.

Interview 5

Mr E came over as a self-assured man who believed that he was doing all that was necessary to help small businesses. His position within the bank relieved him completely of the trivial items that plagued Mr C. He appeared to be wholly concerned with loan applications and the monitoring, in considerable detail, of outstanding loans.

He was willing, he said, to consider any viable proposition, and believed that security was the very last consideration. He seldom declined applications, although he sometimes had to 'twist around a little' an applicant's proposal, 'but only in the interests of the customer'.

Mr E could not see the need for any new schemes, and believed that any approaches from entrepreneurs could be fitted within existing facilities. He viewed the range of publicised schemes with some criticism 'I don't need leaflets to tell me what to do, because I would do it without them anyway.'

Asked whether he had had any involvement in equity stakes, he said that he had not been approached by anyone interested in this form of support.

He was hopeful that the new wave of managers, with the aid of an extremely intensive training system, would eventually bring about changes along the desired lines.

'The way I operate is in line with the way the top boys believe we should be operating. There are lots of whizzkids in London – at the very top – and they are determined to change the image and operations of the bank.'

The way Mr E operated did indeed seem impressive, and he obviously benefited from having the freedom to devote a considerable amount of time and effort to the consideration of business loans.

Were there any areas in which his bank could improve its performance? 'The bank still needs to put itself across better – we are very poor at advertising. People are still afraid to visit their bank managers and we must overcome this.'

Here was a man who enjoyed helping small businesses. Indeed, it was almost as if he vicariously enjoyed the 'thrill' of entrepreneurship through the projects he supported.

'If someone comes here with a good idea, then one way or another I'll find someway to help him,' he asserted.

Conclusions

The findings from this small sample of interviews do highlight the fact that bank managers are themselves *people*. It is quite unlikely that bankers, even those working for the same clearing bank, will give an identical response.

'If I'm too busy, the answer is "no".'
It all depends on how I feel at the time.'

In addition, it would appear that certain lending proposals involving a high degree of risk are turned down by managers who fear they may blot their copybook and thus perhaps miss a promotion. Yes, a manager's own personal objectives may in fact be in conflict with the bank's own objectives.

Although the banks tend to deny that there exists an obsession with security, or that they are far too conservative in their outlook, the interviews produced a mixed response. However, what is clear is the belief that slowly, but surely, change is taking place as a 'new breed' of banker takes over from the 'old school'.

The interviews supported the views of numerous studies 'that small businesses have problems in presenting relevant information in support of their case to bankers'

If bank managers are really to fulfil their role of assisting small firms, they must be freed from trivia and the pressure from above. They need a climate in which they can make the best possible use of their time and talents. In short, bank managers need to manage.

Attitudes of bankers towards lending to the small firms sector are changing and must continue to change.

Is this small sample of interviews a true reflection of the attitudes of practising bankers?

Why not ask your bank manager?

Are the banks doing enough for small firms?

Are the clearing banks doing enough to provide the finance necessary to increase the birth rate and stimulate the growth of the UK's small business sector? Although the practising bank managers when interviewed tended to agree that bankers were still conservative and risk-averse, they were, however, in general agreement that their own particular banks were doing enough to help the small businessman.

Alas, the barrage of criticism still persists. Why, even when banks have introduced numerous new schemes, should they still come under fire?

To obtain an answer to this question and as a follow up to the interviews with the bank managers, interviews were conducted to obtain a neutral view with representatives from the SFIS and the ICFC. In addition two entrepreneurs were interviewed to ascertain any problems that arose in their respective cases.

Small Firms Information Service (SFIS)

This advisory service frequently acts as the 'middleman' between the banks and entrepreneurs and is well qualified to assess the strengths and weaknesses of both parties.

The interview commenced by asking Mr F for his own honest opinion of the ability of banks to carry out small business appraisals. He replied that, sadly, the banks were in his opinion 'not qualified' to make such assessments. He pointed out that when the SFIS recently made new appointments they did not appoint applicants with banking experience as they believed that the applicants, during their banking careers, had not acquired the necessary experience in the area of business appraisals. The training of bankers, he believed, was improving but was still deficient in important areas.

Mr F also detected the continued existence of 'deep-rooted' conservatism.

He referred to the 'belt and braces' approach practised by the banks and considered that a typical branch consisted of either a senior man near to retirement or a young man on his way up, with neither wanting to be seen to make a mistake.

Mr F was sure that the banks' policy-makers were sincere in their efforts to change attitudes but was afraid that their pronouncements were not 'filtering down' to the lower levels.

He pointed out that an entrepreneur's first contact with a bank normally came at the local level and unless the attitude was right at this level then the entrepreneur, unless he was persistent and went 'over the head' of the local manager, was often discouraged from starting up on his own account.

When asked for a final opinion as to whether the banks would ever provide the risk capital on the scale demanded by their critics, his answer was in the 'yes and no' form: yes – because they must if they are to counteract the competition from the other clearers and from the American banks in particular; no – because the conservatism is too ingrained.

He did, however, stress that the future depended on the effects of improved training methods and the success of the policy-makers in bringing about a change of attitudes. The 'way' exists but the 'will' is still weak. Mr F confirmed the difficulties that the banks were having in dealing with all the various services they offered. He described a recent case where a small-businessman with the assurances of the SFIS, had to visit a bank on three separate occasions before he could convince them that they did in fact run the particular scheme that he was enquiring about!

Industrial and Commercial Finance Corporation (ICFC)

The ICFC, with its wealth of experience in the provision of venture capital, is well placed to assess the professional capabilities of banks in this field.

The discussion with Mr G of the ICFC was primarily concerned with the provision of venture capital, an area in which, with some justification, Mr G viewed the ICFC as 'the professionals'.

He felt a certain amount of sympathy for bank managers and the criticisms they received. He compared the ICFC with its concentration and specialisation in the area of providing, in one form or another, venture capital and the banks, whom he now believed were expected to cover too wide an area.

He described the advisory service provided by a leading bank in terms which our dictionary revealed as being quite unsuitable for printing. He cynically stated that advice from advisory services usually comprised suggestions that the businessman should make more use of the banks' other services.

In defence of the banks, Mr G did believe that far too much was expected of them and did not believe they were by any means the sole answer to the problems confronting small businesses. In addition he stated that the banks had acted extremely responsibly during the current recession and, contrary to reports that they were always too eager to withdraw support, his experience was that the banks had on many occasions lost a great deal of money, which they need not have done, by maintaining support for ailing firms.

Mr G was then asked for his views on the role played by the banks in reducing the death rate of small firms by more active involvement. He believed that there was a great danger of being over-paternalistic and believed that it would not be healthy or practical for the banks to become too fully involved. He mentioned the success of management buy-outs, with which the ICFC have become increasingly involved as an example of the usefulness of allowing businesses to fail. The banks could step in and appoint consultants and turn a company round but he believed it was foolish deception to 'battle on' when the product, the management, the market size, etc., were simply not good enough. A healthy economy, he pointed out, needed a high death rate – provided that the birth rate was also high.

As for the birth rate, Mr G believed a series of ICFCs was needed, with the emphasis on professionalism and specialisation in the new venture area. The banks would, he assumed, continue to develop their venture capital services as a result of commercial pressure but there would have to be drastic changes in organisation and temperament before they were anywhere near as efficient as the ICFC.

The usual criticisms levelled at the entrepreneurs were supported by both Mr G and Mr F, e.g. complaints that small-businessmen often approached the banks unprepared and with projects generally not thought through. These were accepted by both speakers as merely statements of fact and did not necessarily present a major problem.

The banks now boast a full array of advisory services and with the additional option of visiting the SFIS, a small-businessman should be able to acquire the necessary information and instruction needed to formalise his plans. Once again the attitude of the bank manager is of the essence and there is the need for a 'let's see what we can work out' approach, rather than 'go home and think it through again'.

The entrepreneurs

The purpose behind choosing these two particular interviewees was to hear the case for the small-businessman as described by two articulate entrepreneurs both fully conversant with the published material on the subject as well as having valuable personal experience.

The feelings of entrepreneurs are already widely accepted. Every week in the national press articles and statements by or about entrepreneurs can be found. The interviews do not attempt, therefore, to break new ground. The entrepreneur's trail is well worn and the interviewees were merely asked to describe their own journeys along this trail.

Solicitor's fitness

Mr H was a solicitor; he had run a successful private practice for four years before deciding to start, from scratch, a fitness centre. In addition, whilst in practice, he had also been involved with some success in other enterprises. The difficulties that Mr H experienced in finding the necessary finance to fund his plans proved to be substantial and would almost certainly have discouraged a person with less perseverance. The long search for backing led Mr H through what he described as a 'Kafkaesque world of banking and institutional inertia'.

Mr H explained that his proposals produced almost complete perplexity in the majority of the bank managers whom he approached. 'Why,' the bankers asked in amazement, 'should a solicitor want to become a gymnasium proprietor?' Pressing further, Mr H reminded the bankers about a particular venture capital scheme advertised by them and was told: 'Oh, that, I don't believe I've heard of a successful applicant under that scheme . . . Don't place too much hope on that – our moves in the direction of venture finance are very tentative indeed. As far as you're concerned all the old rules still apply.'

The 'rules', as Mr H came to appreciate, were: solicitors did not become gymnasium proprietors; banks very rarely lent without collateral; new projects were too risky and not really considered a 'sound' investment. Finally Mr H was left in the catch 22 position of 'get it built and we might look at it.'

Through the introduction of new partners and a second mortgage on his house, Mr H began the project without the help of the banks. At a later stage and only after the costly and extensive conversion of the premises was well under way, did Mr H find a bank – incidentally, not one of the big four – to back his venture. Persistence had proved worthwhile and the gymnasium is currently operating successfully and the intention is to look into the possibility of opening a second one in the future.

It is worth quoting at some length the conclusions drawn by Mr H; 'The most compelling legacy I have received from these experiences is an awareness of the power and the tendency of the banks to asphyxiate good, viable ideas. The business logic, the advance research and administrative planning were all impeccable. Detailed financial data was prepared and we have matched our projections, which proves their accuracy. None of this availed with the big four banks.

'Their system of lending tends to perpetuate existing commercial structures, inhibiting expansion, change and innovation. Their recruitment policy favours cautious and prudent decision makers over the imaginative and enthusiastic. The project nearly died, but is now a thriving business. How many other good ideas, which could create prosperity in jobs, products and services, are being aborted for lack of funds?'

When this particular case was discussed with bank managers their reactions were not surprising:

'It's easy to be wise after the event; it could so easily have been a different story.'

'For every example you quote I can quote an example of a satisfied customer.'

'I know many banks are like that – but not mine.'

'Well, why should a solicitor want to run a gym?'

Apart from one manager, who said he could well understand Mr H's desire to do something entirely new, the general reaction was that Mr H was simply relishing the 'I told you so' smugness of a person who had proved the banks to be wrong in his own particular case.

All this brought home the very subjective nature of reporting interviews and the danger of drawing too many conclusions from individual cases. Was Mr H's preparation really impeccable? Was he lucky to succeed? It is almost impossible to answer these questions and one must rely heavily on personal impressions which the reader is free to take or leave.

However, it must be emphasised that Mr H was in our opinion extremely articulate, intelligent, thorough-minded and, above all, determined and, in short, the type the banks stress they are eager to meet. He was genuinely concerned about the 'pool of talent' being wasted in this country as a result of the treatment received by innovators and entrepreneurs at the hands of the banks.

In a final comment spoken with more than a slight trace of desperation, he asked: 'If I, with my training, systematic preparation, dogged persistence and enthusiasm, can encounter such difficulties over what proves to be a profitable venture, then what sort of chance does a budding entrepreneur have with what may be a brilliant idea but with possibly less ability in articulating his case? Without collateral he may as well give up!'

From large to small

The final interview was with Mr I, a man who can hardly be described as a 'typical' entrepreneur. Mr I left a large firm to start a small business that now prospers and has grown to medium-size status with growth still envisaged. In addition to his own entrepreneurial activities, however, Mr I is also heavily involved in lecturing and running courses for small businesses. Mr I has not only personal experience of entrepreneurs but also a thorough knowledge of management theory and practices. It must be emphasised that the choice of interviewees was intended to investigate the views of what the banks would normally be expected to consider as 'model' entrepreneurs. Any difficulties that they experienced would, one assumes, be compounded for someone with less experience or knowledge.

Mr I was quick to point out the problems caused by the fundamental difference in temperaments between entrepreneurs and bank managers. In addition the differences in temperaments are aggravated by what Mr I believes is a lack of experience on the part of bank managers in actually running a business. He believed that a banker could never really comprehend the problems faced by an entrepreneur. He was also critical of bank managers for a concentration upon the present and historical track record of a firm and stated quite frankly that there was a general inability to assess future developments, market trends and performance projections.

After hearing, on so many occasions, the accusation that entrepreneurs approached banks without well-thought out plans, it was strange to hear an entrepreneur state that his own plans were often too advanced and sophisticated for bank managers to comprehend.

Whilst criticising the banks on certain aspects, Mr I did believe that he had received a good service over the years from his bank. The success with which he regards his partnership with his bank must largely be accredited to his 'text book' presentations and his policy of maintaining close communications with his bank. Periodic meetings with frank discussions, in which Mr I admits difficulties as well as successes, have resulted in the establishment of mutual trust.

On the question of security, Mr I was in sympathy with the banks. It was obvious that he was a hard bargainer and the interview did reveal that banking rules can be bent or stretched if the entrepreneur has the confidence, skill and experience to present his own case forcefully.

Conclusions

Mr F of the SFIS expressed the view that bankers were incapable of carrying out business appraisals and confirmed the findings of the interviews with bank managers, that bankers do have problems in keeping pace with all the new schemes and services provided by their banks.

Should bankers be recruited by the SFIS? A banker could well help to bridge the 'information gap' and 'knowledge gap' that exist between banker and small business. This could be particularly useful in the area of assisting the small man in presenting his case to the bank.

Mr F's comments were supported by Mr G of the ICFC: 'The banks are expected to cover too wide an area.' Mr G's opinion that a high death rate of small firms is healthy is not as bad as it sounds, provided that there is a healthy birth rate. Businesses have to make the best possible use of scarce resources, so why fund a 'lame duck'? The banks could well be found guilty of maintaining support for ailing, inefficient firms and starving new high potential growth firms of funds. Yes, they could be accused of killing off the 'goose that lays the golden egg' and failing to make a contribution vital to the future prosperity of the UK.

If a capable entrepreneur is having problems attracting finance then surely there must still be something wrong with the existing banking structure.

Bank managers – 'old school or new breed'?

In recent times the banks have been subjected to a barrage of criticism for their failings in meeting the financial needs of small firms. It was in this context that we held interviews with five bank managers from large northern city branches to ascertain what they felt about their own relationships with the small business sector in the UK. The interviews were designed to obtain the *manager's* view as opposed to the official view. It was, however, too much to expect managers to talk in general terms as their own experience and views depended very much on the attitudes, facilities and environments within their own banks.

It is extremely difficult to analyse in tabular form the responses of the managers to the various questions posed. The table does attempt to summarise the replies to certain key questions, but for a clearer understanding we must examine what the individual managers actually said.

| Question | Answer | | | | |
	Mr A	Mr B	Mr C	Mr D	Mr E
1 Are managers conservative by nature?	Yes	Yes and No	Yes	Yes	Yes and No
2 Is security essential for a new venture?	Yes	No, but	Yes and No	Yes	No
3 Should the banks have equity holdings in small companies?	No	Yes	Yes, but	Yes	Yes, but
4 Are term loans adequately covered?	Yes	Yes	Yes	Yes	Yes
5 Have the banks too many schemes?	Yes	Yes	Yes	Yes	Yes

Conservatism

Although A said 'yes', he was convinced that in the south younger managers working in a more commercially vibrant environment could be less conservative. B did not agree about geographical location affecting conservatism, but did agree that age was an important factor. This was supported by C who said, 'You can't change the habits of 30 years', and E who believed that there was still a lot of 'deadwood' in the system.

- Are younger managers less conservative in their outlook?
- Can an old dog learn new tricks?
- Have the banks failed in the continuing education of their existing managers?

Education is and always will be a continuing process; a manager worth his salt should strive to keep abreast of current developments. This, however, is not enough: the manager's commitment should be matched by a commitment to continuing education by his/her employers.

Security

Managers appeared to be in agreement that security reflected commitment and provided an incentive on the part of an entrepreneur. B admitted that he would be worried about someone who was reluctant to put up security. It was apparent that banks are still risk averse by the various comments that were made, such as:

- D Without a personal knowledge of customers, how can an advance be made without security?
- A What they don't realise is that it is not our money. We have a responsibility to our depositors and shareholders.

It was also evident that change on this front is taking place. Although C considered that managers were risk averse out of the fear of failure he sensed a more liberal attitude to risk being slowly accepted. E, however, was prepared to consider any viable proposition, security being the last consideration.

The wind of change

The interviews did reveal that slowly but surely the traditional conversative image of bank managers and attitudes to risk are changing. B pointed out that a 'new breed' of managers was beginning to emerge as a result of a more diverse and complex training system.

- C The people at the top – and I mean London – are very determined but we are a large organisation and change takes time.
- D If a banker doesn't occasionally back a loser he cannot possibly be operating in the right areas.

In addition, B stressed that in his view there was very little to choose between the main clearing banks in terms of facilities and schemes and that the *principal differences were between individual bank managers*. Bank managers are people, people are complex and are quite likely to respond in various ways. This view was supported by the interviewees:

- C If I'm having a bad day or I have too much work I'm inclined to say 'No'.
- D I tend to regard it as my money and I don't like to lose it. Do we really want more small businesses?
- E I don't need leaflets to tell me what to do.

Equity schemes

Although the majority were in favour of equity holdings in small companies, they also pointed out that they had little or no experience of this and that in certain cases this form of support was dealt with by their venture capital subsidiaries.

Relationship with regional office and head office

Some of the managers expressed a <u>contempt</u> for the people at regional and head office and considered that their banks had become too bureaucratic and impersonal.

- C I'm encouraged, from above, to go out and visit places and sit down with clients and give help, but it's often just a case of handing them a leaflet.

  The regional office often rejects the projects that I submit, but they don't know the customer as I do.

  The people over there are afraid of making a mistake when they are moving on in a year or two.
- D We get thousands of new things passed down to us and quite often I only have time for a cursory glance.

  There is downward pressure caused by top level determination to become less security conscious at grass roots level.

The interviews highlighted the difficulties of attempting to 'graft on' new functions to an existing organisational structure without tackling the serious personal and organisational problems that may ensue. The banks have, over the years, become rather like large oil tankers. They take a considerable amount of time to change direction. The banks have not been able to make the rapid transitions necessary to satisfy their critics. UK business needs to invest not just in new fixed assets, but in organisational efficiency.

The major problems

What do bank managers see as the major problems affecting small businesses?

- A There is a lack of professionalism, they are aware of how much they need now, but have no idea about future requirements.

- *B* The banks' services are quite adequate, their real problems arise as a result of bureaucratic controls, regulations and taxation.

  The accountants that they employ fail to introduce effective control systems.

More help for the small business?

A and C felt that more personal visits to new and existing customers, backed up by specialist advice, was a step in the right direction. When questioned about their own bank's advisory service the managers concerned admitted that they didn't know too much about that side of things. This indicates that there could well be a 'communication gap' and that the advisory service is not yet working in harmony with the branches.

There was general agreement between the managers that they were satisfied with their own bank's performance. However, E felt that the banks are still poor on the marketing side.

New schemes

'Just what was needed to counteract the conservatism of certain managers', was how C described the Government Loan Guarantee Scheme. Although most of the managers welcomed this scheme there was unanimous agreement between them that there were far too many new schemes.

- *C* You hear all about these wonderful schemes, but there are just too many to be able to know them in detail.
- *D* Little did I know when I entered banking that I would be required to become an insurance agent, a computer manager, a travel agent and so forth.

And E considered that there was no need for any more new schemes as any approaches from entrepreneurs could be satisfied by existing facilities.

Conclusions

Is this very small sample representative? If it is, then the banks should consider freeing their managers from trivia to enable them to use their time and talents in a more productive manner. Structural changes are necessary for improving organisational efficiency and improving morale.

Continuing professional education for existing managers whether they be 'old school' or 'new breed' is a prerequisite for improving the banks' performance in the long term. In a business environment of economic change and uncertainty the banks must be able to respond more quickly.

It is encouraging to find that the banks have already responded to these challenges. Some banks' managers are being freed from trivia, structural changes are taking place and the education and training of managers is certainly more intensive and demanding than it was, say, 10 years ago.

C strongly believed that the clearing banks were the only organisations capable of doing something to help the small business sector. The relationship between banker and customer is unique and has a vital part to play in bringing about an increase in the birthrate and a slowing down of the deathrate of small businesses. After all, the small firms born today could well be the large firms of tomorrow.

Advice and information for small businesses

A vast percentage of the number of retail organisations in the UK belong to the small business sector and this fact was highlighted in the Wilson Report and Business Monitors, as shown in Table 6.

Table 6: Number of retail organisations in Great Britain 1961–78

| | Organisations (thousands) | | Small as percentage of total |
	Total	Small	
1961	394	374	95
1971	352	338	96
1976	292	276	94
1977	262	254	97
1978	235	224	95

Sources: Wilson Report and Business Monitors, Retailing 1977 and 1978.

Notes
1 A retail organisation may have one or more outlets under the same ownership.
2 Small organisations are defined as those with an annual turnover of less than £50 000 at 1963 prices. This limit was adjusted by the Wilson Committee, to allow for inflation, giving approximate figures of £75 000 in 1971 and £150 000 in 1976. A limit of £250 000 was the only one available for 1977 and 1978, thus making exact comparisons difficult.
3 The 1977 and 1978 figures are based on a VAT-based register of businesses thus excluding businesses falling below the VAT threshold. The number affected was estimated by the Wilson Committee to be 30 000 for 1976, with an average turnover of £3 200 and an average employment of 1.8 persons. This suggests, first, that the recent decline is not as marked as the

figures imply. Secondly, the importance of small organisations is underestimated

A small/medium-sized retail organisation with its limited resources cannot hope to match its larger counterparts in terms of the expertise of staff and the supply of relevant management information.

Evidence presented to the Wilson Committee pointed out that it was often difficult for small firms to put together the kind of presentation needed to successfully obtain finance. This was mainly due to a lack of specialist staff and the fact that an owner/manager may not be very sophisticated financially. This suggested that in addition to information on the finance available there was a need for general financial advice and help. What sources of information and advice are open to the small/medium-sized retailer? Is there a shortage of information and advice for the small business sector of retailing?

At present it is possible to identify four sources from which information and advice may be obtained. These are as follows:

1   Accountants and professional advisers.
2   Financial institutions.
3   Government sponsored bodies.
4   Various trade and business organisations.

A survey carried out by the Association of British Chambers of Commerce in the UK small firms sector included the question 'If you need help, to which of the following would you be most likely to turn?' Replies were received from 3740 firms as follows:

Accountant	1383
Solicitor	561
Bank manager	543
Chamber of Commerce	496
Trade association	485
Business consultant	143
CBI	129

This shows that the sources of information and advice most likely to be consulted were localised and familiar, the accountants, solicitors and bank managers with whom most small firms have contact. An indication of the actual use made of these sources can be obtained from a survey, by R. D. Back of the Small Business Unit of the London Business School. He found that only 2 per cent of owner/managers failed to confer with their accountants at least once a year, whereas 45 per cent failed to confer with their bank managers. Only 13 per cent of those surveyed had financial information, other than annual accounts, prepared by their accountants.

This suggests that many owner/managers are either unaware of the opportunities for advice available to them, or else feel that they have little need for such advice. In recent years much effort has gone into advertising the various advisory services available.

Accountants are potentially the most important source of advice on information for small retailers. Those in practice exceed the total number of branch bank managers. They are familiar to small business men and are consulted far more frequently than bank managers, though this is often because of the legal requirements for audited accounts. Unfortunately, they suffer from the serious disadvantage of not having a formalised, national network. Both the main accountancy bodies have published information on sources of finance. The journals they issue contain articles on small business and detail relevant changes that may affect them. However this is not enough to ensure that all accountants are able to offer a comprehensive advisory service to their small business clients. In view of the contact accountants have with the vast majority of small firms, any improvement in their advisory capacity could have considerable effect. How good is the accountant on the advice front?

The financial institutions are the next most important source of advice and information. This is particularly true of the clearing banks, who again have contact with large numbers of small retailers. They are in a position to reach all small businesses. Over the last few years the quality of the advice that they offer has been greatly improved. It must be recognised that the banks are not an impartial source of advice and will often be interested in providing some form of financial service to those who consult them.

Few of the other financial institutions provide advisory services catering for the smaller business. Most specialise in offering particular financial services and more general information and advice is beyond their scope.

There are a number of government sponsored bodies providing information, advice and counselling services. Their services tend to be of a higher standard than the banks or accountants can provide, but are on a much smaller scale.

The Small Firms Information Service, under the Department of Industry, was set up in response to recommendations made by the Bolton Committee of 1971. This is a purely advisory body and offers information and counselling through its Small Firm Centres in the main industrial towns, and its Area Counselling Offices. In Scotland and Wales the service is run by the respective Development Agencies. Any information provided is free but individual counselling may involve a modest charge.

CoSIRA is the main government sponsored agency assisting small rural businesses. It provides a small, effective and personal service with a strong local commitment. Its counsellors usually have a wide business knowledge and their services are in considerable demand.

In Scotland, advisory services are provided by the Scottish Development Agency and the Highland and Islands Development Board. Wales has the Welsh Development Agency and the Development Board for Rural Wales, an equivalent of CoSIRA. In Northern Ireland the Development Agency runs a Local Enterprise Development Unit which advises small businesses. These agencies will also consider arranging finance.

Critical examination of the available sources of information and advice strongly suggests that an 'information gap' may indeed exist. Accountants lack the formalised framework necessary to provide an adequate service to their clients. The banks, whilst having the ideal framework needed to meet small retailer needs at a local level, are still seen by many purely as a source of finance and their advisory services are ignored. The various government agencies and private business associations offer better counselling and advice, but this is not available on the scale needed. A gap exists in the supply of advice and information at local level and steps should be taken to remedy this.

3

Financial analysis

The final accounts, i.e. the trading and profit and loss account, and the balance sheet of a business, are frequently subjected to an analysis involving the use of accounting ratios. Many analysts, researchers, accountants, students and others who undertake such analysis work, all too often ignore the limitations of the source data and the ratios that are used. This is why three of the following readings take a more critical look at the drawbacks of the source data and the problems which attach themselves to ratio analysis.

However, this chapter does start with a piece of ratio analysis. So, why use it? The reason for using ratio analysis is the quest for a yardstick against which to compare and measure performance. Even given the limitations, doing some ratio analysis, surely, must be better than doing no ratio analysis at all! At least the reading about comparing financial performance in retailing does attempt to be a fair appraisal by using published ratios from a reputable source.

When you have completed this chapter you should be more aware of the limitations of the final accounts (both those published and those used for internal reporting purposes) and avoid the avoidable pitfalls that could occur if and when you become involved in financial analysis.

Comparing financial performance – ratio analysis and retail management

'Is our own company's financial performance good, bad or indifferent?' This frequently posed question is one for which management must strive to find a satisfactory answer. One attempt to provide a yardstick with which to compare one's own company's performance is the publication of industry figures.[1] However, there is quite a time lag between the publication of this information and the years to which it relates. Even so, it is better to have some measure of performance rather than no measure at all. The important thing about financial ratios is not so much the ratios themselves, but the questions which they provoke.

What can financial ratios tell management?

The use of ratios enables comparisons to be made between figures of incommensurable size and therefore acts as an indicator of performance. They provide management with a tool, which when used in conjunction with other data, can be used for evaluating their own company's performance. Ratios may be used to illustrate the broad aspects of financial and managerial performance. They can also be used to help assess the effects of internal and external environmental factors upon the company, e.g. managerial decisions, governmental legislation, economic factors and so on.

Profitability

投資報酬率

ROI (Return On Investment) is the real name of the business game. The productivity of the capital employed is of prime importance. The providers of finance are willing to invest funds in a business provided that they are likely to receive an adequate return on their investment, commensurate with the risk involved. All funds, whether or not they are self generated, have an 'opportunity cost'. It is therefore of great importance that the return on funds invested in a company compares favourably with what could be earned outside. One of the principal reasons why, in recent times, certain UK companies have invested their own funds in US companies has been to secure a better rate of return on their capital!

For the retailing industry as a whole the picture which emerges is not surprising. The returns on capital, assets and for shareholders have all declined as profit margins have had to be trimmed to meet increased competition. This picture is also reflected by the three sectors: Department Stores, High Street Trading and Home Improvements and DIY. On the basis of these figures (Table 7) it would appear that High Street Trading has not suffered from recession quite as much as the others, in that the 1980/81 Return on Capital has gone down by 3.6 per cent compared with 1978/79 and the Return on Shareholders Funds has gone down over the same period by 3.7 per cent. It must also be noted that, using the same two measures, Home Improvements and DIY are getting above the industry's average. The important question for retail management is, how do your own company's figures compare with those of the retail industry/appropriate sector?

a) The return on capital $= \dfrac{\text{Profit before tax} \times 100}{\text{Capital employed}}$

b) Return on assets $= \dfrac{\text{Profit before tax} \times 100}{\text{Total assets}}$

c) Profit margin $= \dfrac{\text{Profit before tax} \times 100}{\text{Sales}}$

d) Return on shareholders funds $= \dfrac{\text{Profit before tax} \times 100}{\text{*Shareholders funds}}$

*Shareholders Funds = Issued paid up Ordinary Share Capital + Reserves.

Table 7: Profitability – ratio analysis

Industry/sector		Department stores			High street trading			Home improvements and DIY			The retailing industry		
Ratio	Years	78/79	79/80	80/81	78/79	79/80	80/81	78/79	79/80	80/81	78/79	79/80	80/81
a) Return on capital	%	18.5	17.8	14.2	18.2	17.3	14.6	19.2	24.6	15.5	18.4	17.9	14.6
b) Return on assets	%	13.2	12.9	10.5	11.9	11.0	9.5	10.3	13.3	8.7	12.2	11.7	9.7
c) Profit margin	%	8.3	7.8	6.8	5.7	5.3	4.5	5.3	7.2	4.8	6.3	6.0	5.0
d) Return on shareholders funds	%	20.3	19.7	15.8	20.9	20.2	17.2	23.2	29.4	18.0	20.9	20.6	16.8

Asset utilisation

This measure of efficiency is all about the relationship between the assets which the company owns and uses, and the generation of sales revenue. The ratios used are:

e) $$\frac{\text{Sales}}{\text{Total assets}}$$

f) $$\frac{\text{Sales}}{\text{Fixed assets}}$$

From the figures (Table 8) it would appear that High Street Trading has the better asset utilisation, i.e. for every £1 of assets in 1980/81 £209.60 of sales were generated, and for the same period for every £1 of fixed assets (e.g. buildings, fixtures, fittings, equipment, etc.) £3.70 of sales were generated, in both cases above the industry average.

Warning! Comparisons of this type are difficult. Some companies may own their buildings, others may rent them, some of the fixtures and equipment may be owned or leased. This means that companies who rent their premises and/or some of their fixtures/equipment will have lower assets/fixed assets and therefore a better utilisation figure.

Liquidity

Liquidity ratios are an indication of a company's ability to pay its debts as those debts fall due. They also provide an insight into the efficiency of the company's control and management of working capital, e.g. credit control; inventory control and cash flow management and so on.

The position revealed (Table 9) for both the current and acid test ratios is one of stability. The liquidity position must be very carefully watched, e.g. an acid test of 0.4 means that for every £1 owing to creditors the company concerned only has 40p's worth of liquid assets as cover. Some companies tend to get so pre-occupied with the business of selling, that other areas such as credit control and inventory control are neglected. A greater investment on resources in these two areas could well assist in improving liquidity and profitability. The rate of stock turnover has tended to increase over the years in question, possibly because of the recession, but this is a step in the right direction.

The Liquidity Ratios were:

g) *The Current Ratio*

$$\frac{\text{Current assets}}{\text{Current liabilities}}$$

h) *Acid Test*

$$\frac{\text{Liquid assets (i.e. Current assets – Stocks)}}{\text{Current liabilities}}$$

i) *Stock Turnover*

$$\frac{\text{Sales}}{\text{Stocks}}$$

Table 8: Asset utilisation – ratio analysis

Industry/sector	Department stores			High street trading			Home improvements and DIY			The retailing industry		
Ratios Years	78/79	79/80	80/81	78/79	79/80	80/81	78/79	79/80	80/81	78/79	79/80	80/81
e) Sales/total assets	158.9	166.2	154.1	207.2	208.4	209.6	194.7	184.3	180.2	192.9	195.6	193.2
f) Sales/fixed assets	2.6	2.7	2.5	3.8	3.9	3.7	7.0	5.8	4.6	3.5	3.6	3.5

Table 9: Liquidity – ratio analysis

Industry/sector	Department stores			High street trading			Home improvements and DIY			The retailing industry		
Ratio Years	78/79	79/80	80/81	78/79	79/80	80/81	78/79	79/80	80/81	78/79	79/80	80/81
g) The current ratio	1.3	1.3	1.3	1.2	1.4	1.1	1.4	1.4	1.3	1.2	1.2	1.2
h) Acid test	0.6	0.5	0.6	0.5	0.4	0.4	0.6	0.6	0.5	0.5	0.4	0.5
i) Stock turnover	7.8	7.8	8.3	8.4	8.1	8.9	5.2	5.0	5.1	7.8	7.6	8.3

Table 10: Gearing – ratio analysis

Industry/sector		Department stores			High street trading			Home improvements and DIY			The retailing industry		
Ratio	Years	78/79	79/80	80/81	78/79	79/80	80/81	78/79	79/80	80/81	78/79	79/80	80/81
j) Debt/net worth		0.2	0.2	0.2	0.2	0.3	0.3	0.3	0.3	0.3	0.2	0.2	0.2
k) Shareholders funds/ Total liabilities		0.7	0.7	0.7	0.6	0.5	0.6	0.4	0.5	0.5	0.6	0.6	0.6
l) Interest cover	%	8.7	11.9	13.8	7.7	10.8	15.0	12.1	11.2	15.8	8.1	11.1	14.7

Gearing

The gearing ratios were: (Table 10)

j) Debt/Net Worth
k) Shareholders Funds/Total Liabilities
l) Interest Cover Percentage

$$\frac{\text{Gross interest paid} \times 100}{\text{Profit before interest and tax}}$$

The picture here is that for the two more highly geared sectors, i.e. High Street Trading and Home Improvements and DIY the interest paid as a proportion of the profits generated has increased more sharply. The reason for this is that interest on loans and debentures has to be made whether or not the company makes a profit. In times of adverse trading conditions it is, therefore, the companies with a high amount of long-term debt that are most vulnerable.

Conclusions

Management may, by comparing their company's financial performance with industry figures, highlight strengths and weaknesses. This should enable them to chart a course into the future aimed at converting those weaknesses into strengths.

Ratios are not an end in themselves, they do suffer from certain deficiencies, but at least they provoke numerous questions and encourage management to find an answer.

How do you compare?

References
[1]*Industrial Performance Analysis*, pub. ICC Information, 8th edition, 1983.

The author acknowledges the substantial amount of useful data contained in three reports on these sectors published recently by ICC Business Ratios, 28–42 Banner Street, London EC1Y 8QE.

Financial analysis revisited: Source data – income measurement

Accountants and others are frequently guilty of placing great store upon the results of a financial appraisal carried out by them, which utilises the audited accounts as the principal source of data. Such an analysis will, from the outset, suffer from the limitations attributable to income statements and balance sheets prepared in accordance with existing accounting concepts, conventions and Statements of Standard Accounting Practice (SSAPs). Yes, possibly the most heavily utilised source of financial data does have serious limitations, limitations which tend to be ignored by numerous financial analysts. There is no doubt whatsoever that such analysts are well aware of the limitations of the source data. However, such analysts also continue to make a lot of use of such data, maybe because it is one of the only sources of information open to them. Some information, whatever its drawbacks, is better than no information at all!

Limitations of the audited accounts

One of the major problems associated with the audited accounts is that they are historic documents. They are based on past figures and look backwards and not forwards! It should, therefore, be appreciated that when faced with the task of forecasting future performance, the historic accounts comprise just one small component part of the information available. To use past performance as a principal predictor of the future is a dangerous occupation. You know very well where you have been, it's where you are going to that is important! A further problem arises as a result of a time lag between a company's year-end and the publication of their results. In the UK time lags of six to twelve months are quite common. This means that the information produced is so out of date by the time it is published that is ceases to be of any real value. Quite a number of companies, to their cost, have found out too late that they were making considerable losses. Thus, the appropriate corrective action that should have been taken, had the facts been known earlier, was not taken, resulting in the liquidation of the company and its assets. Thank goodness that many companies do have regular periodic accounts prepared and also make good use of management accounting techniques which look forwards and not backwards.

The income statement – the measurement of profit

Does the income statement give a true and fair view of the profit? What is *fair* is a subjective judgement and the *view* depends upon where you are standing! Auditors do, in fact, have considerable discretion in the performance of their duties. Firms of accountants may possess widely divergent views upon the application of accounting postulates, concepts, and principles. Thus, a 'true and fair view' which should quite rightly be an objective judgement is really a subjective judgement. It is dependent on the opinions and attitudes of the particular firm of accountants concerned.

Sales (turnover)

The sales figure is not always as straightforward as one would think. Firstly, it could be reported gross or net (i.e. sales less returns). The problems in this area are the result of varying treatments of particular types of sales such as:

a) Hire purchase sales.
b) Goods on sale or return, e.g. mail order firms.
c) Inter-company sales, e.g. groups.
d) Cash and credit sales.

It would be most useful from an analysis point of view if a breakdown of cash sales and credit sales was given, e.g. for credit control analysis.

The *realisation* concept dictates that a sale is a sale when the goods have been delivered and invoiced (say, at the VAT tax point), not when the cash is actually received. The sales figure may include a number of unknown bad debts. Thus, the reported sales figure may be significantly overstated even after making or increasing the provision for bad and doubtful debts. If you are unaware that one of your major customers is about to go bust, you may also experience great difficulty or follow the same route. Yet, your last set of accounts showed a healthy position and you may even have paid tax on the sales revenue represented by the debt from the customer who has gone into liquidation.

The operation of the 'cut off procedure' which will vary significantly from company to company (and possibly from year to year), does affect the reported figures.* It can in fact be used to do a bit of 'window dressing' depending upon the particular display that the company has in mind! If a sale immediately prior to the year end is excluded the items represented by the sale will simply remain in the stock figures but will not appear in sales or debtors until the new financial year. This means that both the sales and debtors figures will be understated. It is not necessarily a 'swings and roundabouts' situation in that last year's 'cut-off' period sales are included this year and this year's 'cut-off' sales are included in next year. Sales in the 'cut-off' period may vary significantly from year to year and their treatment may also vary from year to year.

The cost of sales

Goods purchased are also affected in the same way by the application of the 'cut-off procedure'. Purchases may also be quoted as gross or net. They are included with the reported purchases figure if they have been received and invoiced (say, at the VAT tax point). However, they are affected by the *matching concept* which attempts to offset their cost against the sales revenue in the accounting period in which they are actually sold. Purchases of raw materials, etc., could be described as a 'deferred expense', i.e. an expense incurred now, the benefit of which will materialise when those goods are converted into revenue.

The matching process leads on to a major problem area, that of stock valuation. Companies within the same industry may employ totally differing methods of valuing their stocks of raw materials, work-in-progress and finished goods. One of the principal problems involved with the valuation of work-in-progress and finished goods is how much to include for overheads. This involves many subjective judgements such as:

a) The identification of cost centres.
b) The selection of bases of apportionment, e.g. in proportion to: floor area or cubic capacity or number of employees.

*The *'cut-off procedure'* is the system for dealing with goods coming in and going out immediately prior to the year end to ensure that if goods are treated as sold then they are excluded from stock, included in sales and included in the debtors figure and vice-versa for purchases.

69

c) The treatment of service department costs, administration costs, research and development costs, and selling and distribution costs.
d) The selection of an appropriate overhead absorption (recovery) rate, e.g. direct labour hour rate; machine hour rate, etc.

In addition to the above there is also the problem of selecting a method of inventory valuation such as: FIFO (First in First Out); LIFO (Last in First Out); and weighted average cost. It is specified by the 1981/89 Companies Act that all of the above mentioned methods (and some others) may be used in the charging of raw materials to production. Thus, the most recent Companies Act permits a variety of methods which can be adopted!

The method used for inventory valuation will be stated in the accounting policies section of a company's published accounts. The accounting concept of *consistency* demands that the methods adopted should be the same from year to year. However, if the company does decide to alter the method used, it can do so provided that a note about the change (if material) is included in its published accounts. It must also ensure that its statement of accounting policies is amended. Companies are, therefore, not bound by the consistency concept because company law provides for changes in accounting policies. The other methods referred to above as acceptable by the Companies Act 1981/89 include:

a) The lower of cost or net realisable value.
b) The lower of cost, net realisable value or replacement price.
c) Standard cost.
d) Cost less a provision to reduce the stock to net realisable value.

This brings into play a concept which affects many other figures which appear in the income statement (profit and loss account) and balance sheet, the concept of *conservatism*, e.g. (a), (b) and (d) above. Conservatism in action calls upon businesses to anticipate no profit and to provide for all possible losses.

The 1981/89 Companies Act does provide further help to the analyst/user, in that if the value of stock differs significantly from its replacement price a note disclosing the difference in value should be included with the accounts. Good, but there is still a problem and this is caused by the concept of *materiality*. What is significant? Exactly just what is significant will depend upon many factors, e.g. the amount concerned, the industry, the size, etc., but possibly even more important, the attitude of the person who has to make the decision. People are complex variables and in the area of subjective judgement are quite likely to come up with different solutions and decisions! Apart from the provisions of the 1981/89 Act the historic accounts do not take into account inflation. There will, therefore, tend to be an understatement of the value of inventory in times of rising inflation. Inflation adjusted accounts do go someway towards improving the situation. As a starting point, inflation adjusted accounts take the historic accounts and then adjust them for the effects of inflation. Thus, inflation adjusted accounts still suffer from most of the defects associated with the historic data.

The accuracy of the stock-take is also questionable. There are so many errors that can take place which may significantly affect the reported stock figures. Errors may occur in: counting, (e.g. double counting), omission, pricing (e.g. wrong price), denomination of quantity; treatment of old or obsolete stock; goods on sale or return.

It is quite possible that dozens of companies with identical products and sales volume could have exactly the same quantity of goods in stock, e.g. raw materials, work-in-progress and finished goods, but all have widely differing stock valuations for the reasons explained above. Stock valuation does affect the reported profit!

Expenses

The treatment of expenses in computing the net profit will be affected by the application of the accounting concepts, postulates and principles. It is not the purpose of this article to enter into the debate about the difference between concepts, postulates and principles. From now on, therefore, I will simplify matters by calling them all concepts.

In the area of expenses the concepts interact and conflict. The matching of revenue and expense for a period, e.g. the treatment of accrued and prepaid items may conflict with the materiality concept. So, again, subjective judgement enters into the arena.

It must be remembered that the provision for bad debts (conservatism at work) is just an estimate whether it be general or specific. It may, on occasions, have quite a dramatic impact on the reported profit.

There are a number of deferred revenue expenses which may significantly affect the reported profits, but are still ignored.* Accounts do tend to be prepared for tax purposes, the simple reason why such expenses are not dealt with correctly. At the year-end, a company may have a significant stock of stationery or advertising literature. However, the total expenditure just gets written off during the year in which it is incurred, there being no carry-forward of the stock value into the next accounting period. Also, because of the changes to taxation capital allowances, some companies will be trying to put items which should really be treated as fixed assets in with their repairs and renewals expenses!

Other items worthy of note which present problems when attempting to measure profit include:

a) *Research and development costs*
   The treatment of such costs may vary from including it in product costs to a total write off in the profit and loss account.

b) *Contingent liabilities*
   A contingent liability refers to something that may, or may not happen. The treatment will vary from simply showing it as a note to the accounts to

---

*Deferred revenue expense. An expense, the benefit of which extends beyond the accounting period in which it was incurred.

making a provision to cover its anticipated effect in the profit and loss account. The anticipated effect, e.g. liability under a warranty provided to customers, will be quite difficult to estimate.

c) *Profits on long-term contracts*

The profits on long-term contracts, e.g. construction, first of all have to be estimated taking into account the value of work certified and work not yet certified. Having estimated the profit to date a decision has then to be taken as to how much of that profit should be taken into the current year's profit and loss account. Conservatism tends to manifest itself in this area as it is considered imprudent to take all of the estimated profit to the profit and loss account. This situation arises because of the nature of the industry, there could be a number of unforeseen contingencies. Nevertheless, a decision has to be made on how much needs to be taken to the profit and loss account.

d) *Depreciation*

The treatment of depreciation is similar to that of stock valuation in terms of its inclusion in the statement of accounting policies and any significant changes to the method/s adopted. Accounting for depreciation involves:

  i) Selection of the method to be adopted for each category of fixed assets. Popular methods include: Straight Line Method; Reducing Balance Method and Revaluation Method.

  ii) An estimate of the residual value of the fixed asset if it is intended to take it into account with the selected method. Estimates of the residual value will no doubt vary quite widely.

  iii) An estimate of the life of the fixed asset. The question which must be asked here is, which life? The life selected could be the life as per manufacturer information; the life as estimated by the management of the company acquiring the fixed assets; the life over which the company intends to keep and use the fixed asset and so on.

  iv) Whether or not to implement the recommendations of the SSAP 12, Accounting for Depreciation. This standard does provide for revaluations of fixed assets including land and buildings.

The amount of depreciation charged in the accounts can significantly affect a company's reported profits. It must also be noted that the financial accounting depreciation is usually completely different to the Capital Allowances which are available for tax purposes.

e) *Exceptional Items*

SSAP 6 provides guidance for the treatment of those items which derive from transactions outside the ordinary activities of the company. These items should now be brought into account on the face of the profit and loss account. The Companies Act 1981/89 embodied these requirements into its standard format. Here, also, materiality still plays a part, if the item in question is considered as insignificant, then it will not be shown as an exceptional item.

f) *Taxation*

It must be remembered that the corporation tax figure in a company's accounts is only an estimate. When the corporation tax liability is finally agreed, it could be a lot more or a lot less than the published figure.

It must also be noted that the provisions of the SSAPs are not mandatory unless their provisions have been incorporated in legislation. Companies can, therefore, ignore many of the recommendations contained in the SSAPs.

Other income

Other income such as rental income may need to be apportioned if it extends into the next accounting period, provided that it is material. The treatment of hire purchase interest receivable will have to be decided upon and the amount, if any, of hire purchase bad debts. Dividends received are usually included in the accounting period when they are actually received in cash and not the period to which they relate. This method tends to conflict with the realisation concept.

Conclusions

The income statement (profit and loss account) does suffer from quite a number of drawbacks and limitations. Many of the drawbacks result from the numerous occasions on which subjective judgement has to be exercised. The application of accounting concepts also quite frequently depends upon subjective judgement. Various methods may be selected for dealing with inventory valuation and depreciation. The 'cut-off procedure' may enable companies to do a bit of 'window dressing'. Taxation considerations may dictate how certain items are to be treated, even at the expense of giving a really true and fair view!

Someone once asked an accountant to work out their profit, the accountant replied, 'Yes, I'll work it out for you, how do you want it? High, low, medium, or would you prefer a loss?' It is a fact that the way in which the sales, cost of sales, various expenses, depreciation and taxation figures are computed can significantly affect reported profits.

Financial analysis revisited: Source data – the balance sheet

Much has been written on the meaning and interpretation of balance sheets. So much so, that its limitations may frequently be overlooked, forgotten or simply ignored. A vast amount of research carried out by academics and a considerable amount of information generated by financial analysts/accountants depends very heavily upon balance sheet information. The calculation of ratios and the tabulation of statistics based on balance sheet figures, it would appear, tends to give it a false sense of credibility as a reliable source of information. The users and recipients of the information are quite likely to perceive the balance sheet as an accurate picture of how things are, and could place too much reliance on it. The information which is extracted can only be as accurate as the original information upon which it is based. If the source data has serious limitations, the analysis of such data also suffers from those limitations.

Textbooks and articles on the subject of understanding and interpreting balance sheets devote little or no space to a serious discussion of its limitations. This further adds to the perception of it as some sort of dependable accounting statement. I fear that this is also true of accountancy education. Students usually devote a considerable amount of time to the analysis and interpretation of accounts and balance sheets, e.g. in projects, assignments and case study work. No doubt, the limitations are covered but such coverage is possibly far too scanty. The pre-occupation of working out the ratios and interpreting them, even in conjunction with other data, tends to lead the limitations into obscurity. So, just what are all these so-called limitations?

The balance sheet will never ever show a picture of 'how things are'. The information from which it is derived is *historic*. Thus, it does at least attempt to show 'how things were'. It is not a statement of economic or realisable values but one of *historic costs*. History looks to the past and is usually not an accurate predictor of the future! The income statement discussed in the first article in this series covers a particular historic period, the balance sheet is even more limited than this. The balance sheet just shows the position at a particular moment frozen in time. It has been likened to a snap shot, e.g. take one today – a picture of health, but take one tomorrow – a picture of woe! Another problem is the delay between the balance sheet date and the publication of that balance sheet. A period of several months may elapse between the balance sheet date and its ultimate publication. Therefore, the information is quite out of date by the time it is received and 'a lot of water' will no doubt have 'flowed under the bridge' during that time. By the time the information is published, the position could have changed quite significantly. The Companies Act 1981* does require publication of known significant changes (Box

---

Box 1 The directors' report must disclose:

a) Information about the business development of the company and its subsidiaries as follows s.13(3):
   i) *A fair review* during and at the end of the financial year, e.g. turnover, profits, taxation, trading conditions, markets.
   ii) *Important events* which have occurred since the year end, e.g. trading conditions, acquisitions, competition.
   iii) Likely *future developments*.
   iv) *Research and development* activities.
b) Particulars of the acquisition and disposal of its own shares, by any company (private or public), s.14.

---

*The provisions of the Companies Act 1981 have now been consolidated in the Companies Act 1985/89.

1) which occur after the balance sheet date. However, what is significant is a matter of subjective judgement and, in this particular area, discretion usually rests with the company's auditors. Also, the statement may be in the hands of the printers by the time the significant changes come to light.

The balance sheet only shows those items which can be measured in monetary terms. Quite a number of factors which cannot be measured in monetary terms are not shown in the balance sheet. Such factors may considerably influence the viability and successful operation of the company, e.g. the morale of the work force; the ability of the management team; the location; future prospects, and other qualitative factors.

The Companies Act

The Act did attempt to improve the situation relating to uniformity and rules for computing figures.

Part 1 of the Act, s.1–21, prescribes the *format* and *contents* of the published accounts of companies and *rules* for computing the figures which appear in those accounts.

Companies must now:

a) Publish a balance sheet using one of two statutory formats (see format 2, pp. 76–7).
b) Prepare their published *profit and loss account* according to any one of the four statutory formats.
c) Adopt historical accounting rules which, with one or two exceptions, tend to follow existing practice, but they may adopt any of the alternative accounting rules contained in 1 Sch. 29–34.
d) Provide more information in the *directors' report*, See Box 1 opposite.
e) Include much more information in the *notes to the accounts*.
f) Ignore certain provisions contained in the Act if doing so means that the accounts will show a true and fair view, s.1(1).
g) Still continue to publish a section dealing with *accounting policies*.

However, the legislation still lacks bite in that it still relies on subjective judgements for all the items listed (a) to (g) above, e.g. which format to adopt? Which accounting policy? Which method of valuation?

There is also another balance sheet format which may be adopted, i.e. Format 1.

Fixed assets – intangible and tangible

There are a number of ways in which development costs may be dealt with in the accounts. They may be absorbed into product costs and therefore included in stock valuations, written off completely in the profit and loss account or purely written off over a number of years. The treatment will affect the reported profit and loss and balance sheet figures. The methods adopted for dealing with items such as patents, licences and trade marks also vary. The Companies Act (1 Sch. 31(1)) allows intangible assets (other than good-

75

Balance sheet format

Format 2 (Companies Act)

ASSETS

A Called up share capital not paid

B Fixed assets

  I *Intangible assets*
    1 Development costs
    2 Concessions, patents, licences, trade marks and similar rights and assets
    3 Goodwill
    4 Payments on account

  II *Tangible assets*
    1 Land and buildings
    2 Plant and machinery
    3 Fixtures, fittings, tools and equipment
    4 Payments on account and assets in course of construction

  III *Investments*
    1 Shares in group companies
    2 Loans to group companies
    3 Shares in related companies
    4 Loans to related companies
    5 Other investments other than loans
    6 Other loans
    7 Own shares

C Current assets

  I *Stocks*
    1 Raw materials and consumables
    2 Work in progress
    3 Finished goods and goods for resale
    4 Payments on account

  II *Debtors*
    1 Trade debtors
    2 Amounts owed by group companies
    3 Amounts owed by related companies
    4 Other debtors
    5 Called up share capital not paid
    6 Prepayments and accrued income

  III *Investments*
    1 Shares in group companies
    2 Own shares
    3 Other investments

  IV *Cash at bank and in hand*

D Prepayments and accrued income

LIABILITIES

A Capital and reserves

   I *Called up share capital*

   II *Share premium account*

   III *Revaluation reserve*

   IV *Other reserves*

      1 Capital redemption reserve

      2 Reserve for own shares

      3 Reserves provided for by the articles of association

      4 Other reserves

   V *Profit and loss account*

B Provisions for liabilities and charges

      1 Pensions and similar obligations

      2 Taxation including deferred taxation

      3 Other provisions

C Creditors

      1 Debenture loans

      2 Bank loans and overdrafts

      3 Payments received on account

      4 Trade creditors

      5 Bills of exchange payable

      6 Amounts owed to group companies

      7 Amounts owed to related companies

      8 Other creditors including taxation and social security

      9 Accruals and deferred income

D Accruals and deferred income

will) to be shown at their current cost. A further complication to an already complicated situation.

The valuation and treatment of goodwill is one of the most controversial issues in accountancy. Although it is ignored completely by numerous ongoing concerns, clearly it is of value. How should goodwill be valued? There are many methods which may be utilised and writers on the subject will possibly never reach agreement on which method should be adopted. Valuation of goodwill is a problem, but so are the later decisions which must be taken about whether or not to write it off in whole or part.

In the case of consolidated accounts, goodwill is usually calculated as follows:

	£000	£000
Cost of shares acquired		250
Less		
Nominal value of shares acquired	150	
Add		
Pre-acquisition profits		
(applicable to Holding Co.)	75	225
Goodwill arising on consolidation		25

The above figure of £25 000 is perhaps better described as cost of control. However, whatever it is called does not alter the fact that there will be a multitude of reasons for the difference, e.g. expected future earnings, market values of fixed assets, dividend policy, property revaluations before the acquisition, etc.

Tangible fixed assets such as land and buildings, plant and machinery, fixtures, fittings, equipment and motor vehicles may be worth a lot more or a lot less than their book value. These assets are usually shown at their historic cost less depreciation. Cost is a fact, but nevertheless only an indication of value at the date of purchase. There are several methods which may be selected as appropriate for the charging of depreciation, e.g. straight line, reducing balance, revaluation, etc. Subjective judgement is also involved, e.g. in the estimation of the asset's life and scrap value. The Companies Act alternative accounting rules (1 Sch. 31(2)) permit companies to adopt market value or current cost for the valuation of tangible fixed assets.

The SSAP 12 on Depreciation does attempt to put right some of the defects of historical cost concept accounting. It encourages and permits the revaluation of fixed assets, e.g. land and buildings and the re-assessment of an asset's life. However, revaluations are not an easy matter, valuers will not always agree to a particular value. Also, an asset's life expectancy is still just a matter of opinion. The picture is further clouded by the renting or leasing of fixed assets. This most certainly presents comparability problems, e.g. Firm A owns its own land and buildings, Firm B rents its land and buildings.

The cost concept also affects investments. The Companies Act further complicates matters. It permits companies to adopt alternative accounting rules (1

Sch. 29–34). In the case of investments held as fixed assets, companies may include them at their market value or a director's valuation (1 Sch. 31(3)). The trouble with market values is that they may fluctuate greatly from day to day. Director's valuations are highly subjective and the assumptions on which they were based may change overnight.

There is also the added complication of deciding upon whether an investment is long-term (held as a fixed asset) or short-term (held as a current asset). Assessments about this will vary and circumstances may change, e.g. short-term investments may change to long-term investments and vice-versa.

Current assets

The drawbacks relating to stocks as described in the first article, e.g. methods of valuation, treatment of overheads, cut-off procedure, conservatism, etc., have an impact upon the position disclosed in the current assets section of the balance sheet. In addition, the Companies Act also provides that stocks may be shown at their current cost. The stock figures as at the date of the balance sheet may be totally unrepresentative of the real levels of stock which have been held throughout the year. Yet, quite a number of ratios used by analysts/ accountants make use of these stock figures!

Another area which could have been subjected to 'window dressing' is debtors. The debtors figure, as at the balance sheet date, may also be unrepresentative of the level of debtors which actually existed throughout the year. The company may have had a purge immediately prior to their year end to collect outstanding debts and/or may have excluded some year end credit sales from debtors via the operation of their 'cut-off procedure'. The provision for bad and doubtful debts can significantly affect the reported debtors figure.

The use of unrepresentative figures for stocks and debtors must surely lead to poor quality decision-making and unsound conclusions.

Investments held as current assets will also be shown at their historic cost. The Companies Act Alternative Accounting Rules, however, enable companies to have them valued at their current cost. The cost of an investment will tend to fluctuate from day to day. By the time the balance sheet is published the investment's value may have changed significantly or it may have been realised.

Liabilities

Capital and reserves

The called-up share capital is shown at its nominal value. The reserves may have been affected by a revaluation of fixed assets, e.g. land and buildings as follows:

a) Never!
b) This year or last year.
c) Several years ago.

Quite a number of business people are unwilling to revalue fixed assets simply because their reported ratios will look worse! If the profit is expressed as a percentage of a higher base figure the ROI (return on investment) is going to be lower than it would have been had there been no revaluation!

The profit and loss figure, representing the profits ploughed back over the years suffers from all the drawbacks which were mentioned in connection with the income statement.

Provisions

The taxation figure is only an estimate. When the computations are finally agreed with the Inspector of Taxes (i.e. several months after the company's year end) the amount of liability could have changed significantly. The actual liability is not usually known at the date on which the accounts are actually published and cannot, therefore, be communicated.

Creditors

Debentures, bank loans and overdrafts may be long-term or short-term. In fact, in the case of an overdraft, part could be hardcore debt and part could be fluctuating and flexible debt. Further reasons why financial analysis is such a difficult task, if it is to be objective and if it is to give a 'true and fair' view.

An improvement introduced by the Companies Act was to distinguish clearly between trade creditors and other creditors. When they were lumped together it was impossible to get an accurate calculation of the average payment period being taken. As with stocks and debtors, creditors as at the balance sheet date could be completely different to the levels which existed throughout the year. The operation of the 'cut-off' procedure also affects creditors.

The section on accruals and deferred income is influenced by subjectivity, materiality and the application of the matching concept. A change in audit personnel could well lead to a change in the application of the concepts.

Monetary liabilities

Historic balance sheets do not take inflation into account. Monetary liabilities such as debts due and creditors will, in times of rising inflation, be worth much less, in real terms, than their book value! This is because as inflation rises the purchasing power of the pound decreases.

Reporting exemptions for small and medium-sized companies

The Companies Act provides that small and medium-sized companies are exempt from filing certain documents and information *with the Registrar of Companies*. Thus, the information which is available to the external user is reduced.

Small companies s.6

Small companies *may file* a *modified balance sheet* but *need not file*:

a) A profit and loss account
b) The Directors' report
c) Details of higher paid employees and directors' emoluments
d) Certain notes, e.g. accounting policies etc. s.6 (2c & 5)

Medium-sized companies s.6

Medium-sized companies *may file a modified profit and loss account* but *do not* have to disclose certain items by way of note.

Conclusions

For many of the items disclosed in the balance sheet there are a number of alternative figures which could have been included. Even legislation adds to the complexity by first of all, permitting choices and secondly, by the inclusion of the word 'may'. The SSAPs relevant to balance sheet preparation and reporting are not mandatory. Whatever the method used to compute the figures, the principal drawback of any balance sheet is that it only shows the position as at a particular moment in time. In a world of swift and fluctuating environmental change, by the time such figures are reported they are likely to be way out-of-date.

How can academic research and financial analysis be justified, when the source data suffers from so many serious limitations?

Accountants, analysts, researchers, students and others must devote more time and effort to assessing the limitations of the balance sheet. For internal comparison purposes the data has much greater validity. Whereas for external comparison purposes the problems are multiplied, e.g. different companies with different interpretations of the application of accounting concepts and methods of valuation.

What must be done?

More must be done by way of CPE (Continuing Professional Education) and via the education of existing/future accountancy/business students (examiners please note!). To my mind, there is just too much flexibility, too much reliance on the balance sheet at the expense of other data, and not enough carefully thought-out legislation.

Financial analysis revisited: Ratio analysis – a critical appraisal

The first two articles in this series concentrated upon the limitations of the income statement and balance sheet. Their reliability as source data was examined. During the questioning process, one word cropped up time and time again, subjectivity! The final accounts are highly dependent upon subjective judgement relating to: methods of valuation of assets; the operation of the 'cut-off procedure'; the application of accounting concepts and the interpretation of legislation, etc. This somewhat unreliable data source is used quite extensively by accountants, analysts, researchers and students in their attempts at financial analysis and intepretation. One of the principal uses of the data in the quest for meaning and understanding is ratio analysis. The usage of the data for ratio analysis purposes, it would appear, tends to give the data some sort of 'perceived respectability'. However, as with computers, it is still really a question of 'GIGO' (i.e. Garbage In, Garbage Out)! The ultimate results from the analysis can only be as accurate as the original data. This, therefore, the third and final article, takes a critical look at ratio analysis and the difficulties of securing meaningful comparability.

There is much to commend an internal analysis within a company or group of companies. The final accounts will be more uniform from year to year. The application of the accounting concepts, methods of valuation, etc. will be more consistent. Unpublished information can also be utilised. The analysis can take place at more frequent intervals, e.g. quarterly. Management can set the yardsticks (i.e. targets) with which to compare performance. However, external analysis is a different 'kettle of fish' – it is in fact a 'minefield'! One hears accountants and others say, 'Oh yes, but to derive meaning from this ratio, we must take a look at the appropriate industry figures'. This sounds quite a reasonable course of action in the attempt to produce a 'yardstick'. First of all the industry figures will not tell us whether the ratio is good, bad or indifferent. Secondly, quite a number of companies included in a particular industrial category may in fact be highly diversified!

There are also a number of other practical considerations which affect external comparability, the principal ones being:

a) *Year ends*. Companies listed as belonging to a particular industry are quite likely to have different year ends. Thus, variances must surely arise which reflect the differing economic conditions which existed during the periods covered.

b) *Annualisation*. Figures may be produced for periods in excess of 12 months. To aid comparability such figures are converted into their annual equivalents. This assumes that the revenues, profits, etc. have been earned at a uniform rate throughout the period. This is an unlikely event and further distorts comparability.

c) *Size*. If you compare a dwarf with a giant you will end up with a large variance. The industry figures will contain the results of large, medium and small companies. For a more realistic comparison, it would make more sense to compare with companies of a similar size, e.g. based on turnover.

d) *Nature*. As mentioned above, companies may be highly diversified yet listed under a particular industry category. The nature may also vary in terms of production methods, products, and selling and distribution methods. For example, one company may sub-contract its distribution function, another may own all of its own vehicles.

e) *Location*. Quite a number of variances may be the result of differing cost structures applicable to differing areas, e.g. the impact of incentives, expensive rates, proximity to motorways/ports and airports.

f) *Asset financing*. Alternatives to the outright purchase of fixed assets include sub-contracting, leasing and hire purchase. It is difficult to make comparisons between companies who own their land and buildings with those who simply rent them or have a combination of the two. Adjustments to the figures may be made to facilitate comparison, but such adjustments are highly subjective. The problem becomes even greater where fixed assets such as plant and machinery, motor vehicles, fittings and equipment are concerned. The degree to which companies will use leasing, sub-contracting, hire purchase or outright purchase will be subject to numerous combinations and tremendous variations.

In addition, the picture is further complicated by the revaluation/non-revaluation and depreciation of fixed assets as indicated in the second article.

Therefore, if you have to make an external comparison select a firm/firms which: are in the same industry (e.g. with a similar product range); are the same size; employ the same type of selling and distribution methods; adopt similar methods for financing their assets; use identical/almost identical accounting policies; are located in a similar area and who have the same year end. Extremely difficult!

Accounting ratios

The accounting ratios suffer from: the inadequacy of the source data; a shortage of source data (i.e. published information); variety in definitions and methods of computation; and variety in formulae.

Many textbook-type ratios are used with such great frequency that their validity tends to go unchallenged. They, too, have earned a form of 'perceived respectability.'

What is wrong with the ratios?

a) **Profitability**

i) *Return On Capital Employed (ROCE)*

For a kick-off, terminology. This ratio is also called Return On Assets, Return On Investment, Profit Ratio and, no doubt, other names as well.

$$\frac{\text{Profit before tax} + \text{Loan interest (long term)}}{\text{Issued capital} + \text{Reserves} + \text{Loan capital } less \text{ intangibles}} \times 100$$

There are many other alternative ways of calculating a Return On Capital Employed, e.g. using after tax and/or after interest figures. What is long term? Some authorities favour two years, others much longer periods. This adds to the complexity, and affects the amount of interest which has to be included. Should a bank overdraft be included in the figures? Some say yes, some say no! The profit may or may not have been adjusted for exceptional items. What is exceptional is open to differing interpretations!

The base figures used are usually those which exist as at the end of the year which is being reviewed. This means that the profit generated during the period is being expressed as a percentage of the investment at the end of the period. It is accepted that profits are being generated throughout the period, many of which are being ploughed back and re-invested. It is, however, most unlikely that the profits will have been earned at a uniform rate throughout the year. The amount invested (i.e. the base figure) at the beginning of the year could also be used, but still suffers from the ploughing back/re-investment phenomenon.

Other defects arise from the difficulty in measuring profits, and the revaluation of fixed assets. The revaluation of fixed assets may have a significant effect upon the reserves.

An approach which adds a little common sense towards providing a better solution to the dilemma calculates the ROCE according to who requires the information, e.g. ordinary shareholders, directors, creditors, etc.

ii) *Profit Margin* (Profit/Sales Percentage)

$$\frac{\text{Profit before tax} + \text{Loan interest (Long-term)}}{\text{Sales}} \times 100$$

Again, one must ask which profit figure should be used? Should it be after tax and/or after interest?

The base figure, sales, is by no means straightforward. It is affected by the operation of the 'cut-off procedure' and the treatment of returns, hire-purchase sales and goods on sale or return.

iii) *Return on assets*

$$\frac{\text{Profit before tax} + \text{Loan interest (Long term)}}{\text{Total assets}} \times 100$$

This ratio depends upon the book valuation of the assets, a highly dubious figure. The fixed and current asset book values may be way out of line with their real worth. There are many variations and formats to this type of ratio, e.g. using manufacturing fixed assets; different profit figures.

b) **Asset utilisation**

i) *Sales to Total Assets*

$$\frac{\text{Sales}}{\text{Total (or Fixed assets)}} \times 100$$

Both lots of figures used for this have already been questioned and their deficiencies highlighted.

ii) *Stock Turnover*

$$\frac{\text{Sales}}{\text{Average stock}}$$

The average stock is computed by adding the opening and closing stock figures together and dividing by two. The two stock figures could be totally unrepresentative of the levels which really existed throughout the trading period. Also, the stock is valued at cost. A more realistic stock turnover figure could be computed by dividing cost of sales (excluding labour costs) by the average stock. This would mean that the stock turnover figures would no longer be affected by mark-ups.

c) Liquidity

Should the bank overdraft and/or certain short-term investments be included in the working capital? The outcome of this decision will affect the liquidity ratios. Include the bank overdraft and the ratio is more adverse!

i) *The Current Ratio*

$$\frac{\text{Current assets}}{\text{Current liabilities}}$$

ii) *The Acid Test (Quick Ratio)*

$$\frac{\text{Current assets less stocks}}{\text{Current liabilities}}$$

Both of these ratios are known by a number of other names. The figures are also affected by accruals, prepayments, provisions for bad debts, proposed dividends and estimated taxation, all of which are highly subjective in addition to the problems described in the earlier articles relating to the valuation of stocks. Comparability between different companies in this area is extremely difficult and resultant ratios should be treated with caution.

In certain industries stocks may, in fact, be more liquid than debtors, e.g. the hotel and catering industry. This calls for a modification to the way in which the above mentioned liquidity ratios are computed. This point is appreciated in the real world, but how many users, analysts, accountants and students fail to grasp its significance?

Some of the leading authorities in this area favour the inclusion of quoted investments in with the current assets figure. The inclusion of quoted investments will improve the liquidity ratios.

iii) *Debtor Turnover and Average Collection Period*

$$\frac{\text{Sales}}{\text{Average debtors}} = Debtors\ turnover$$

$$\frac{365\ \text{days}}{\text{Debtors turnover}} = Average\ collection\ period\ (in\ days)$$

The sales figure which should be used should be the credit sales figure. This credit control ratio is all about the efficiency with which outstanding debts (for *goods sold on credit*) are collected. The Credit Sales figure is not published, so the analyst has to make the best of a

85

bad job by using the wrong figure, i.e. Total sales (which covers cash and credit sales).

The debtors figure, as with stocks, may be completely unrepresentative of the position which existed throughout the year under review.

iv) *Cash flow*

Cash flow = Retained profits plus depreciation

Depreciation is added back because it is a non-cash transaction. However, profits are affected by quite a number of other non-cash items, e.g. provisions for bad debts, adjustments to stock valuations, accruals, prepayments, proposed dividends and estimated taxation. The calculation may also include/exclude exceptional and extraordinary cash/non-cash items! The SSAP 10 Funds Flow Statement goes a long way towards indicating where the cash came from and went to during the year. Having said that, this statement does not take into account the numerous non-cash items listed above.

d) **Gearing**

There are so many different gearing ratios about that it is quite a task selecting those which are most appropriate.

Gearing will be affected by: the treatment of the bank overdraft; property revaluations, i.e. increases in the reserves; dividend policy; the measurement of profit, i.e. its affect upon the retained profits; hire purchase and leasing; and the interpretation of what constitutes long term and short term.

In the coverage ratios, conflict arises as to whether profits should be before or after tax.

e) **Employees**

Whether it be profit per employee, sales per employee, fixed assets per employee, etc. in addition to the problems associated with profits, sales and fixed assets, etc. there is the added complication of computing the average number of employees. This is quite a difficult task because it has to take account of leavers, new employees and part-time employees. It fails to take into consideration variances arising from sub-contracting, production methods and other practical differences.

f) **Growth**

The principal argument against growth ratios is that they tend to ignore inflation. Reported growth increases could, in real terms, be negative growth!

Conclusions

Why use the published accounting data? The simple answer to this is that for external comparability purposes there is nothing any better! Some data, even with the drawbacks enumerated, is better than no data at all.

Why use accounting ratios? There always has been, and will continue to be, a quest for a 'yardstick', i.e. an objective measure of performance. Ratios can be used in conjunction with other data, they provoke rather than answer questions and over a number of years can be used to identify trends. They may also be regarded as giving warning signals, e.g. the need to improve inventory control and credit control. There are, nowadays, very good computerised databases which provide ratios for companies/industries. They do their best to ensure that the data published is as comparable as possible, given the limitations of the source data. They may make a number of adjustments to take account of, e.g. property owned – property rented; fixed assets owned – fixed assets leased, etc.

Will it help to predict the future? If we could find satisfactory measures for predicting the future we would all be backing horses! The data from which the ratios are computed are still just historical records. They were never intended to be an indication of future performance and were prepared to meet legal and taxation requirements. There has been academic work carried out into the predictive power of ratios. Whatever their results, I remain very sceptical because of the serious limitations of the source data and of the ratios themselves.

As mentioned, internal analysis and comparison is far superior to external analysis and comparison. This is because, internally, more data is available and it has been prepared on a consistent basis.

Where do we go from here? The most recent Companies Act has taken a step in the right direction towards improving uniformity of presentation and calculation. More information needs to be published if ratios are to be accurate, e.g. credit sales, average stock per month, average debtors per month and so on. It ought to be possible to make comparisons on a regular basis and not just at some time way after the year end.

The accountancy bodies need to spend more time on areas such as: The adoption and application of concepts; A standard system of accounting ratios; Introducing guidelines to avoid the abuses of 'window dressing', e.g. the operation of 'cut-off procedures', etc.

The Government could help by introducing legislation which cuts down the amount of subjectivity exercised by those who prepare the published accounts.

Who ever thought that the accounts would provide them with a true and fair view?*

---

*Chadwick, L. 'A True and Fair Analytical View. (A concise appraisal)' *The Accountant* 14 August 1985.

4

Working capital management

This is an area which numerous texts on finance and accounting tend to either ignore or devote very little space to. The inspiration for many of the readings in this section was sparked off by an American called H. N. Woodward who said that, 'frequently your best source of finance is hidden in your balance sheet'. Hence my voyage of discovery with articles such as 'Buried treasure' to identify hidden sources of finance. This led me to look very carefully at an area which I describe as internal finance which is generated in addition to retained earnings or can add to the retained earnings. The readings cover the major aspects of working capital management and look at the ways in which production and marketing management can assist. They also take a look at the role of audit (internal and external) in the control and management of working capital.

Another of the areas which numerous authors tend to ignore is holding costs. The readings included in this chapter not only attempt to define what holding costs are but also suggest ways in which they can be reduced.

Having read the articles in this chapter of the book you ought to have a clearer understanding of why working capital management is so important. You may also be able to identify areas in your own or client organisations which could generate some internal finance!

You should find the final reading in this section quite amusing. It tells you what accountants think about marketing management and what marketing management think about accountants!

Should we be more inward-looking for that extra finance?

'Lack of concern with cash flow and the productivity of capital can be fatal to the small company that is on its own. Your best source of capital is often hidden in your Balance Sheet.'[1] Unfortunately, when a company needs more finance it tends to look automatically towards external sources of capital, e.g. an immediate appointment to see the Bank Manager. What in fact it ought to be doing is to make better use of the funds that it already possesses. The provision of finance may be described as a system of costs and risks. Obtaining finance from external sources is quite likely to involve the company in a higher cost of capital (when compared with internally generated finance), and also result in higher risk to the company, e.g. a legal obligation to pay interest; some loss of control – bankers vetting company investment plans. Capital is an extremely precious resource and must be used wisely. ROI (Return on Investment) is the real name of the game. Business is all about acquiring capital, investing it, and endeavouring to earn a return greater than the cost of capital.

Balance sheet extract

Balance sheet as at 31 December, 19—			
EMPLOYMENT OF CAPITAL	£	£	£
Fixed assets			
Land and buildings			
Machinery and plant			
Equipment			
Fixtures and fittings			
Motor vehicles			

So, where are all those hidden sources of finance?

Surplus Fixed Assets

If a Fixed Asset such as Plant and Machinery is not being used in the business or has become obsolete it is tying up capital which could well be used for other purposes. Management must ask the question 'Have we any Fixed Assets surplus to requirements?' The answer to this question is by no means simple and would no doubt involve a very careful review of all Fixed Assets. If there are any surplus Fixed Assets, then sell them. Far better to convert the asset into cash and use the cash to finance essential company investment.

One method of creating additional production capacity and which could also lead to the existence of surplus Fixed Assets is the introduction of Shift Working. Although additional labour payments for working unsocial hours and increases to overheads would of course have to be ascertained and taken into account.

A rationalisation programme will also render a number of Fixed Assets available for sale. International Science Industries, a USA company, took over a company owning five plants. Within one year it closed two of the plants, sales remained unchanged, but costs declined by a substantial amount.

Another area in which important savings can arise as a direct result of a *strategy of surplus asset recognition and disposal* is the recreation of Factory and Office space (expanding without rebuilding), for company use. If the additional space is not required then it may be possible to improve cash flow by selling or sub-letting it. This would bring about a reduction in overheads such as rates, insurance, light and heat, etc.

There are no hard and fast rules relating to the above strategy. Only with careful consideration and consultation can management establish whether or not there are any surplus fixed assets. It is a task in which all members of the management team must participate and become deeply involved. This should ensure that all managers are vigorously involved in the Financial Management of their company simply by getting the best out of the limited resources at their disposal.

The replacement of Fixed Assets

What is the machine going to do? Quite a simple question for management to answer, but all too often companies end up by purchasing a machine with uncalled for capability. Why expend capital upon an additional gadget which may never be used? The same is also true where a supplier offers a large discount for buying two items of plant and machinery instead of one. In addition to taking up valuable factory space, other dangers are the possibility of creating over-capacity and an increase in overheads. This is yet another example of using up finance which could have been used elsewhere in the organisation. Thus, there is also the 'opportunity cost'* to consider.

Another factor worthy of consideration is whether or not the supplier will take the old machinery or equipment in part-exchange, as the allowance negotiated may be far greater than the asset's scrap value. This would save finance and contribute towards an improvement in cash flow.

Can you justify tying up capital in expensive equipment, when there are competent sub-contractors available? Sinclair Radionics Ltd[2] were able to plough back a vast proportion of their profits to finance their Research and Development effort as a direct consequence of employing the services of sub-contracting firms.

What are the financial advantages of using sub-contractors? There are quite a number. Firstly, the company's investment in Fixed Assets including buildings is drastically reduced. Overheads are reduced. The risk of plant becoming obsolete is born by the sub-contractor[†] and not the company. If you have no machine then it will never become obsolete. Thus, the company can concentrate on the areas in which it has established a differential advantage over its competitors, e.g. Research and Development, Distribution, etc. Savings would also ensue as a result of the company not having to carry stocks of certain raw materials. They would not, therefore, have to incur the holding costs associated with the raw materials concerned, e.g. storage, insurance, etc. The company will possess greater flexibility to enable it to change direction more speedily to meet the needs of a changing business environment. It is a far easier task to change a sub-contractor than to change the whole of an existing production line. A company is rather like a large oil tanker, it takes time to change direction, however if it cannot change direction quickly enough it could become a total write-off. Lastly, there may be a time lag

*Opportunity Cost – The income which could have been earned by investing the Capital in an alternative.

†The company may be required to buy certain tools, patterns and dies, etc.

between receiving finished goods/components from sub-contractors and payment. This period of credit may provide the company with time in which it can sell a substantial quantity of the goods it has received on credit.

Should we buy or lease a Fixed Asset?
Leasing instead of buying will certainly improve cash flow and British Leyland are very careful to point this out in their Leasing Maintenance Package. British Leyland also point to savings in administrative time, greater flexibility, simplification of budgeting, and tax advantages. They even include a recovery service. Leasing is certainly a hedge against obsolescence.

Inflation
It must be remembered that certain Fixed Assets, in particular property, are likely to be worth considerably more than their Balance Sheet value. This should enable the company to obtain more finance from external sources by providing the company with additional security.

Conclusion

Management must strive to identify surplus Fixed Assets and convert them back into cash. 'Search and ye shall find'. There must be a concerted effort by all the management team, and their review should cover *all* the Fixed Assets of the company (note that surplus assets can also exist in Administration, Selling and Distribution).

The employment of sub-contractors and the leasing of assets are both worthy of consideration by management when faced with the replacement decision. The cash flow benefits and greater flexibility could well prove to be essential for a company's long term survival.

Efficient use of fixed assets = Efficient financial management = Increased return on investment

References
[1]Woodward, H.N. 'Management Strategies for Small Companies', *Harvard Business Review*, January/February 1976.
[2]Brown, Rosemary. 'The Sinclair Syndrome', *Management Today*, June 1977.

Internal sources of finance: Inventory and debtors

Efficient management and control of working capital can generate a considerable amount of internal finance. It is wiser to make better use of the funds that a firm already possesses than to obtain more finance from external sources. It can often happen that a firm's inventory and debtors contain a certain amount of hidden capital.

Inventory items

A strategy of surplus asset recognition and disposal[1] also applies to inventory. Management must search out and identify obsolete and scrap items. This strategy will not only result in an inflow of cash to improve liquidity but may also release valuable storage space and contribute towards a significant reduction in overhead, e.g. insurance and other holding costs. The storage space vacated could be used to store materials for expanding product lines or given over to production or may even be available for sale or sub-let.

Stock represents 'capital tied up in goods', quite an old saying, but even more relevant in today's complex and diverse business environment. Thus, if stock holdings can be reduced, the amount of capital tied up can also be reduced.

It frequently happens that, once maximum, minimum and re-order levels have been established, they remain in force for a considerable length of time (see Fig. 4.1). Inventory management needs to review carefully the levels set at regular intervals and also take account of seasonal fluctuations in the production demands for certain components. A more realistic saw tooth diagram could look something like Fig. 4.2.

Management would thus be keeping inventory levels to a minimum throughout the year but in so doing would also take into account the risk of production coming to a halt because of 'stockout'.

The ancient cost and management accounting argument of centralised v. de-centralised stores can also provide useful ideas relating to inventory management. Consider the case of two identical factories producing identical products. Factory 1 has one main store (A) and three sub-stores (B, C and D) whereas Factory 2 has just one central store. Both factories stock component XYZ as in Table 11.

It can be seen that Factory 1 is more likely to carry higher stocks for the simple reason that each sub-store and the main store have their own maximum, minimum and re-order levels for each item of stores. The additional administration and re-handling costs involved by employing a decentralised

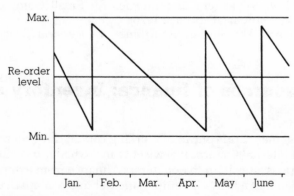

Fig. 4.1 *Saw tooth diagram (Economic order quantity model)*[2]

92

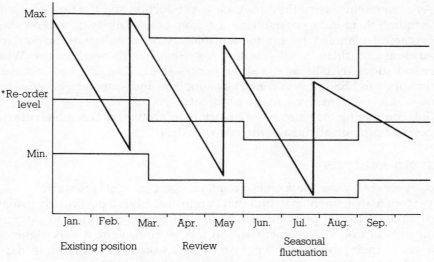

Jan. | Feb. | Mar. | Apr. | May | Jun. | Jul. | Aug. | Sep.

Existing position   Review   Seasonal fluctuation

*This system would involve variations in the re-order quantity

Fig. 4.2 *Effect of review and seasonal fluctuations.*

Table 11: Inventory levels – centralised vs de-centralised stores

Component XYZ	Factory 1		Factory 2	
	Max	Min	Max	Min
A Main stores	20	8		
B Sub-stores	4	2		
C Sub-stores	3	1		
D Sub-stores	3	1	Central	
Total stock holding	30	12	stores 25	6

stores system may even outweigh the time savings attributable to such a system.

How about a system where suppliers carry certain stocks for you?

It may be possible to introduce a system where suppliers deliver certain components on a daily or weekly basis.[3]

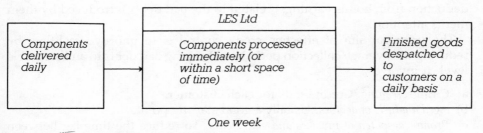

One week

Fig. 4.3 *Regular delivery-despatch system*

As components arrive they are used in production and the flow continued by sending them out to customers on a daily basis. This system depends on very careful planning by production management and co-ordination with marketing and finance. Of course the system has its weaknesses. Where demand suddenly falls or if a strike occurs at LES Ltd, the only course of action open to LES Ltd is to contact its suppliers and suspend deliveries for a time which could involve penalty payments.

Sub-contracting may also reduce stock holdings where the sub-contractors concerned provide all/most of the raw materials.

Pareto analysis

Twenty per cent of your stock could account for eighty per cent of the value[4]
Inventory management may find that Pareto analysis is a particularly valuable technique. If the 20 per cent can be identified and subjected to extremely stringent control, management will in fact be controlling a very significant portion of their stock, e.g. 80 per cent of the value of stock held. It may be possible to introduce a stock grading system which takes into account various factors such as value, importance in production, re-order period, level of service, etc., e.g.

Stock grade	Control frequency
A	Daily
B	Weekly
C	Monthly

The degree of control exercised in this system being determined by the importance of each item of stock.

Debtors (accounts receivable)

Often the quickest and best source of cash[5]
How many credit controllers try to ascertain why a debtor has not paid? Frequently the reason for non-payment can be attributed to mistakes by the supplier, requiring some form of corrective action, e.g. problems regarding quality supplied, damaged goods, etc.

Sales executives receive a commission on sales and could on a number of occasions be guilty of selling to customers who are high credit risks. True, a sales executive is not a financial analyst but some form of penalty (e.g. a deduction from bonus earnings) related to the bad debts introduced by them merits attention.

The principal aim of effective credit control is to improve cashflow by reducing the average collection period and keeping bad debts to an acceptable level. It involves:

a) *Credit screening.* Credit limits for each customer.
b) *Aged analysis of debtors.* Usually a good starting point.
c) *Prompt despatch of invoices and statements.* To reduce the time lag between delivery of the goods and payment. Many firms will not pay until they

receive a statement. Why not increase the frequency with which statements are sent out? Knowledge of your customers' payment systems could enable you to present invoices/statements in time for their next pay-out!

d) *System of chasing slow payers.* Telephone calls (verbal abuse to accounts department may not jeopardise goodwill!), letters ending up with legal action.

e) *Suspension of deliveries.* Can damage goodwill.

f) *Employment of debt collection specialist,* e.g. to collect from hire purchase debtors.

g) *Discounts for prompt payment.* Why use them as an inducement for an already prompt payer?

h) *Surcharges.*

i) *Contra.* Why don't you purchase goods on credit from your debtor and then offset the debt?

Improved credit control not only increases the speed at which cash flows into the business but is highly likely to reduce bad debts. What good is it if you make a sale but fail to ascertain your customer's credit worthiness and you don't get paid?

Cost-benefit

The costs of improving inventory control and credit control must not exceed the benefits to be derived from instituting those improvements. It is a most unsatisfactory state of affairs which permits debtors to avoid payment simply because the cost of collection exceeds the amount outstanding.

The constantly changing environment in which the firm operates dictates that management must always keep a watchful eye on whether or not it is worthwhile to insure against bad debts, to make use of debt factoring or to use book debts as security for a loan.

The role of internal audit (and indeed external audit) should not be underestimated in the control of working capital and the generation of internal finance. By ensuring that adequate systems of internal control are instituted and are operating correctly, losses due to errors and fraud can be minimised. The prevention and detection of error and fraud are particularly important in the area of inventory and debtors. Random stock checks and vetting of authorisation procedures certainly have a moral effect on employees. Internal control is a management responsibility.

Conclusions

The inventory and debtors figures which appear in a firm's balance sheet could well include 'hidden capital'. Unfortunately this can be a direct consequence of inefficiency and management may be reluctant to put right a situation for which they are responsible. Management must strive to reduce stock holdings without endangering the flow of production, as this will reduce capital invested in stocks and release valuable factory space and possibly reduce overheads. Improvements in credit control vetting and collection procedures are considered to be one of the quickest ways of generating cash.

Efficient control of working capital = Improved productivity of capital

References
[1]Chadwick, L. 'Should We Be More Inward Looking For That Extra Finance?' *Management Accounting*, February 1980, page 15.
[2]Weston, J. F. and Brigham, E. F. *Managerial Finance* (British Edition, Holt, Rinehart and Winston, 1979).
[3]Chadwick, L. 'The History of Holset Engineering 1952–1977'. MBA Dissertation, University of Bradford 1977.
[4]Zimmerman, G. W. 'The ABC of Vilfiedo Pareto', *Production and Inventory Management*, September 1975.
[5]Woodward, H. N. 'Management strategies for small companies'. *Certified Accountant*, August 1976.

Mail order inventory control

It is perhaps a useful discipline to remind ourselves every working day that business organisations survive only through satisfying the needs of consumers. As Kotler says 'The key task of the organisation is to determine the needs and wants of target markets and to adapt the organisation to delivering the desired satisfactions more effectively and efficiently than its competitors.'[1]

The catalogue mail order companies seem to be meeting two main needs:

a) Provision of goods with interest free credit. 'Nine out of ten sales are made on instalment credit without extra charge for interest' (Freemans PLC).[2]
b) The convenience of selecting goods at home and of subsequent delivery.

Both the above points have figured prominently in the advertising aimed at the recruitment of new mail order agents.

The satisfaction of consumer needs is the background against which policies on inventory levels have to be made. This reading examines some of the special problems faced by the catalogue mail order companies in the control of their inventories.

Inventory control problems

Mail order companies face the problems of any retailer in the control of inventory, including:

- Setting customer service levels
- Delivery scheduling of incoming goods, both in respect of timing, and batch sizes
- Storage and handling
- Security
- Large number and variety of lines. For mail order companies this is in the

96

region of 25 000 lines when size and colour options are taken into account and when both the catalogue and special offer leaflets are considered.

The specific problems of inventory control for mail order companies result from their method of trading, see Fig. 4.4.

a) Stock is sent to the mail order agent on 14 days approval. While it is out on approval the stock is outside the immediate control of the companies. Approximately 25 per cent of the goods sent on approval are returned unsold to the companies. This means that the returns from agents become one of the major sources of stock which will be used to meet orders placed by other agents.

b) The two leading independent catalogue mail order houses – Freemans PLC and Grattan PLC each have in excess of 500 000 agents. Some of these agents will not follow the normal terms of trading and hence the timing of returns is uncertain.

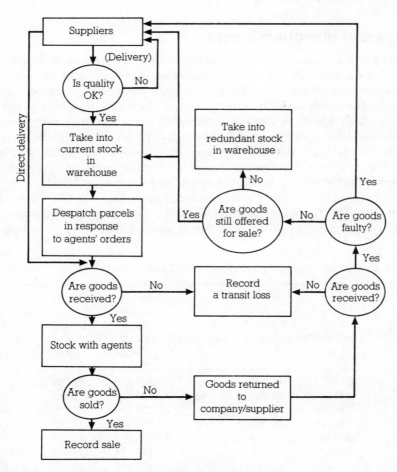

Fig. 4.4 *Outline of the catalogue mail order merchandise flows*

c) Approximately 70 per cent of the catalogue lines are discontinued at the end of one catalogue. Warehouse space and order picking systems mean that the lines which have been dropped cannot be handled alongside the new catalogue merchandise.
d) When a mail order customer orders an item from a catalogue he/she expects to receive that item. If the customer is told that the item is out of stock then a certain amount of goodwill is lost. This situation is somewhat different from a customer going into a department store where he/she can only select from the merchandise displayed at the time. Being in stock on all lines appears, therefore, to be more important for a mail order company than for other retail outlets.
e) Certain stocks are despatched direct to the mail order agents by the manufacturers or suppliers rather than being held in stock by the mail order companies. It should be noted that this method of trading frees mail order firms from investing more capital in stocks and also from having to pay out expensive holding costs.

Comparing inventory levels

Freemans and Grattan have between them a 23 per cent share of the catalogue mail order market.[3] The companies are of similar size, with Freemans currently being the larger. Van Horne reminds us that 'for a given level of inventory, the efficiency of inventory control affects the flexibility of the firm. Two essentially identical firms with the same amount of inventory may have significantly different degrees of flexibility in operations due to differences in inventory control. Inefficient procedures may result in an unbalanced inventory – the firm may frequently be out of certain types of inventory, and overstock other types, necessitating excessive investment'.[4]

A comparison of inventory levels between Freemans and Grattan is shown in Table 12. The figures show that over the last six years Freemans have operated from a lower stock base but have still managed to out-perform

Table 12: Inventory comparison – Grattan PLC and Freemans PLC

Year	Freemans			Grattan		
	Sales (Excl VAT) £000	Closing inventory £000	No. of days sales in stock	Sales (Excl VAT) £000	Closing inventory £000	No. of days sales in stock
31.1.76	126 815	16 550		120 216	21 206	
31.1.77	130 644	20 592	52	137 517	27 455	65
31.1.78	154 839	24 748	53	154 739	27 188	64
31.1.79	186 016	28 190	52	175 602	33 147	63
31.1.80	208 457	37 319	57	213 432	42 770	66
31.1.81	229 434	34 199	57	199 534	27 979	65
31.1.82	257 424	40 444	53	177 101	37 145	67

Grattan in sales turnover growth. During this period of time Grattan have had on average approximately eleven days' extra sales in stock than Freemans. If we apply this average figure to the stock at Grattan at 31 January 1982 then the value of the extra stocks carried as compared with Freemans is approximately £6.1 million. If we assume a cost of financing rate of 15 per cent and other holding costs (storage, space, handling, management etc.) of 10 per cent then the cost to Grattan of carrying an extra eleven days' sales in stock, compared to Freemans, is as follows:

	£000
Financing Costs	915
Holding Costs	610
Total extra costs	1525

The above comparison is purely between the two companies and does not imply that Freemans' performance is at an optimum level. We feel, however, that our comparison highlights the enormous savings which can be made through careful control of inventory levels.

Methods of controlling inventories

It can be argued that a distribution activity, including the need to hold stocks of goods for sale, is the result of effective marketing. In this context inventory control needs effective forecasting of future patterns of trade.

Forecasting stock requirements
In mail order this forecasting which is partly or wholly computer based takes into account order and returns patterns based on previous experience with similar merchandise updated by the actual performance to date of the specific line once it has been offered for sale. In order to get early information on likely demand patterns various techniques are used such as:

- Analysis of orders from preview catalogues issued to staff, and selected agents.
- Analysis of early orders for the new catalogue.

Controlling stocks on approval
Control of inventory which is out with agents is, with the control of debtors, the major challenge facing the catalogue mail order operator. Whilst previous trends of returns may be useful in the forecasting of re-order quantities it is the actual goods themselves which have to be controlled at the operational level. The agency accounting systems are computer based and this allows for a certain amount of automatic reminding, coupled with control reports relating to overdue stocks on approval for review by staff and management.

Handling surplus stocks
These may be handled in a variety of ways including:

- special sale leaflets of previous catalogue goods

- sales to staff
- bulk disposals to market traders
- charitable disposals.

Conclusions

The share of all retail sales taken by the mail order sector has increased from 4.7 per cent in 1976 to 6.4 per cent in 1982, with a projected growth to 6.8 per cent.[5] It is against this background of success in satisfying consumer needs that the challenges of inventory control must be considered.

Our work indicates, from the comparison of Freemans and Grattan, that there are significant differences in the levels of stocks used to support the trading operation. It is significant that Freemans, with a lower overall stock base, has also out-performed Grattan during the last five years in both sales turnover and profit growth, suggesting a more effective control of the balance of the inventory, with associated significant savings in stock holding costs.

References

[1]Kotler, P., *Marketing Management, Analysis, Planning and Control*. (Prentice-/Hall International, 1980).
[2]Freemans PLC, Annual Report and Accounts to 31 January 1981.
[3]*The Guardian*, 15 October 1981.
[4]Van Horne, J. C., *Financial Management and Policy*. (Prentice/Hall International, 1972).
[5]Retail Management Development Programme.

The costs of holding stocks

When asked the question 'how do people set a value on the cost of holding stocks?' one eminent purchasing executive replied 'This is a question to which I have never really found a satisfactory answer. I have posed the question to numerous accountants and the net result was one that could only be described as useless from the point of view of practical application.'

It is rather surprising that many accountants are not particularly interested in this very important area especially when one considers the substantial amount of working capital tied up in stocks of materials and fuel, work-in-progress and finished goods (Table 13).

The stocks held at the end of 1978 by manufacturing industry were a staggering £30.7 bn (around 56 per cent of UK stocks). Figures of this magnitude illustrate how important it is to control stocks effectively.

In most industries the cost of material forms a significant part of the final selling price of the product.[1] Management must not only strive to increase the productivity of labour but must also endeavour to increase the efficiency of Material Requirements Planning (MRP) and thereby improve the productivity of capital. ROI (Return on Investment) is the real name of the game of business. The cost profiles of British industry indicate the importance of materials (Table 14).

100

Table 13: The distribution of UK stocks (at the end of 1978)

		£bn	%
Manufacturing:	Materials and fuel	10.7	19.4
	Work-in-progress	11.7	21.3
	Finished goods	8.3	15.1
Agriculture		4.9	8.9
Wholesale trade		7.2	13.1
Retail trade		5.7	10.4
Other industries		6.5	11.8
		55.0	100

Source: *National Income and Expenditure*, 1979 Edition.

Table 14: The average cost structure of British industry sales

	%
Materials	56
Labour	23
Overheads	14
Profit	7
	100

Source: *MRP and the Organisation* by J. B. S. Houlihan[2]

Thus, other than increasing the selling price which may be sensitive to competition and external factors, materials management may, by direct inventory reduction and increased efficiency, play its part in increasing the productivity of capital employed.

The principal aim of materials management is to keep stocks at an acceptably low level consistent with the risks involved.[3] However, stockouts can cost the firm dearly in terms of lost production, idle time and lost orders. The setting of stock levels and levels of service must therefore involve a trade-off, hence the need for up to date information, continuous monitoring and frequent review.

Holding costs

What is the cost of holding stocks in your company/industry?

A rule of thumb puts the cost of holding stock for one year in the region of 25p for every £1 of stock held.[4]

101

The rule of thumb does indicate that holding costs comprise a significant portion of business expenditure. However, it must be remembered that there will most certainly be quite wide variations between the holding costs of companies and industries.

Which figures need to be included in the calculation of holding costs? It can be observed (Fig. 4.5) that holding costs of stocks include the costs of acquisition, storage, controlling, handling and rehandling, administration and others such as insurance and financial charges, and all these are in addition to the cost of the stocks held.

Fig. 4.5 *The costs involved in holding stocks*

Acquisition costs

The principal cost in the procurement of bought out stock items is the cost of the purchasing function which is made up of staff wages and salaries, office accommodation and equipment and overheads, e.g. light and heat, telex and telephone, stationery, etc. All the costs of ordering, finding suitable suppliers and negotiating terms should be included.

Receiving department costs of personnel and resources used for receiving and inspection of goods inwards may also be classed as part of acquisition costs.

The stores–warehouse function

The stocks of raw materials, work-in-progress and finished goods all take up valuable factory space in terms of expense and scarcity. Factory and office space is nowadays an extremely expensive commodity and must be utilised efficiently. The overheads associated with the space used for storage are many and include: rent and rates, insurance of buildings and equipment, light and heat, fire prevention, cleaning and maintenance. To this must be added the wages and salaries of stores and warehouse personnel. There is also a substantial investment in stores–warehouse equipment, e.g. bins and racks.

In addition there are also losses attributable to shrinkage, deterioration, obsolescence and pilferage to consider.

Inventory control

A lot of time and effort should be devoted to this area in order to keep stock levels to an acceptable minimum and thus bring about savings in holding costs.

The costs applicable to this area involve material requirements planning, monitoring and review, the chief element being manpower. The expenditure upon internal audit related to stock control should also be included under this heading. The cost-benefit of the system of inventory control should not be overlooked.

Handling
There could well be quite a hefty investment in handling equipment, e.g. overhead cranes, etc. In addition to the capital outlay for such equipment further expenditure has to be incurred to cover running costs, maintenance and servicing, e.g. drivers' wages, power, fuel and lubricants.

Administration
It may be more appropriate to include certain expenditure which could quite rightly appear under this heading, under some other heading, e.g. management of purchasing and material requirements planning. However, the costs of the financial and cost accounting recording systems for stocks acquired/issued and payments to suppliers must be accounted for.

Others
a) *Insurance*

   Insurance premiums paid out to cover stock losses cannot be ignored. Insurance premiums are almost certain to rise when a firm increases the value of the stock it holds during the year. As already pointed out insurance must also be taken out to cover buildings, equipment and other risks, e.g. employer's liability and public liability.
b) *Set-up costs*

   Where a company manufactures some of its own components this involves a number of other costs in addition to the direct materials and labour, e.g. setting costs, machinery, patterns, etc. and an appropriate share of overheads.
c) *Imported materials*

   Various fees, duties, freight charges, and foreign exchange management relating to the importation of stock comprise yet another addition to the calculation of holding costs.
d) *Stock out costs*

   The cost of being out of stock can be very high in terms of lost production, sales, future orders and profit.
e) *The cost of capital*

   Stock represents capital tied up in goods and capital has to be paid for, e.g. interest charges and dividends. After all, it should be noted that capital does have an opportunity cost.

Conclusions

The calculation of a company's holding costs is not an impossibility. Holding costs can be identified and classified under a number of headings (Fig. 4.5). However, without actually calculating a company's holding cost it is almost certain that a vast sum of money is expended in this area and that because there are numerous variables the holding cost is unique for each individual company.

Companies do keep an analysis of their payroll and materials used and should therefore be in a position to calculate with accuracy some of their holding costs. Overheads can be allocated and apportioned to departments/cost centres according to established cost accounting practice.

It must be remembered that as stocks increase in volume, value and variety the complexity of management planning and control also increases, and thus holding costs escalate.

References
[1]Lockyer, K. G., *'Factory and Production Management'* (Pitman).
[2]Houlihan, J. B. S., Proceedings of 13th BPICS European Technical Conference, 1978, 103.
[3]Oliver, S. *'Accountant's Guide to Management Techniques'* (Gower).
[4]Ray, D. L., *'Inventory Management Performance Must Improve'*, Purchasing and Supply Management, April 1980.

The reduction of inventory holding costs

If the value and volume of stock held can be reduced, savings should be possible as follows:

a) Interest charges – less capital tied up, less finance required for holding stocks.
b) Storage space – less space required. Substantial savings in rent, rates, insurance, light, heat and personnel.
c) Insurance – lower premiums to cover a lower value held in stock.
d) Capital equipment requirements and associated revenue expenditure reduced, e.g. running costs, interest charges.
e) Handling – better utilisation of capital equipment, e.g. more frequent deliveries. However, this area should be looked at very carefully as handling charges in certain cases could increase.

How can the value and volume of stocks held be reduced?

There are several courses of action open to management. However, it is appropriate at this point in the proceedings to stress the dangers of reducing stock levels. The first danger is that if this resulted in a 'stockout' the firm could be penalised for late delivery and lose future orders. Secondly, the value of stocks held may appreciate in value in times of high inflation to such an extent that the stock appreciation exceeds the holding costs. Thirdly, if materials are ordered in smaller quantities and the frequency of delivery increased, discounts may be lost and certain handling charges increased. There is also cost-benefit to consider. The cost of making savings in holding costs should not exceed those savings. Finally, there are no easy decisions in business, only trade offs and what works for one firm may not work for another.

A reduction in inventory levels may be brought about by:

a) *Surplus assets*
   A strategy of surplus asset recognition and disposal. Stocks which may never be used could be sold and cash flow improved. The same goes for capital equipment which is surplus to requirements. Why invest in assets and incur holding costs when the holding could be forever?

b) *Pareto analysis*
   'Twenty per cent of your stock could account for eighty per cent of the value.' If management exercises more effective control over the 20 per cent they are in fact controlling a vast proportion of the value of stock held.

   Pareto analysis can also be applied to retailing, e.g. 'Twenty per cent of sales could account for 80 per cent of profits.' So, identify those profitable fast moving lines.

   Stock may be graded as 'A' items, 'B' items, 'C' items and so on. 'A' items being the ones which are controlled most carefully, e.g. those which would cause immediate production holdups, fast moving profitable lines, those with long lead times and so on.

c) *Coding and classification systems*
   Firms have been known to place orders with outside suppliers for components which were lying idle in their own stores because of deficiencies in their coding and classification system!

d) *Regular deliveries/stock with short lead times*
   If stocks can be delivered on a regular basis, e.g. daily/weekly and go directly into the production process this reduces the raw material storage space required quite dramatically. This also applies to finished goods in cases where it is possible to despatch daily/weekly to customers, e.g. the motor components industry.

   In the case of stocks which can be obtained at relatively short notice, e.g. hours/days the risks of a 'stockout' are not so serious. Why have large stocks of materials which could be obtained at a moment's notice?

e) *Matching* (JIT).
   With various computer packages available it is becoming more and more possible to match stockholding with production requirements. Obviously this is one of the main aims of materials management. Once a dream, now a reality for certain types of business enterprise. Stock what you are going to use and sell. This calls for close co-operation between materials management, production and marketing. It is no use having a warehouse full of products for which there is no demand.

f) *Variety reduction*
   Variety is expensive. Variety of components stocked increases complexity, e.g. administration.

   One bus company had several different types of automatic doors fitted to their buses. Their stock holding value increased because they had to carry several different door gears and a wider variety of spares. Therefore the use of standardised components can bring about quite remarkable savings.

g) *Review of maximum, minimum and re-order levels*

The stock levels referred to should be reviewed at frequent intervals in order to take account of seasonal fluctuations. In the real world the level of activity in the production departments will vary from week to week/month to month. Therefore the stock levels should also vary, again in an attempt to match materials requirements to production requirements. Some firms set maximum, minimum and re-order levels and then leave them in operation for periods in excess of one year!

h) *Sub-contractors*

The make or buy decision also has implications for holding costs. If goods are bought out finished this reduces: the space needed to store raw materials and work-in-progress; the equipment and operatives required and the associated overheads, e.g. light, heat, etc. The risk of being left with a large volume of obsolete stock is reduced. The employment of sub-contractors is certainly a hedge against plant obsolescence, for it is the sub-contractors who have to provide the production facilities.

i) *The location of stores*

Where a company opts for a decentralised stores system it is quite probable that its inventory levels will be higher than they would be with a central stores system. The reason for this is simple. With a decentralised system the main stores and each sub-store will all have their own maximum, minimum and re-order levels (see Table 15).

The decentralised system also means increased complexity, e.g. increased paperwork – internal orders, etc. and higher costs attributable to rehandling. The trade-off in this particular case is the time saved by having the stores in closer proximity to the production departments. However, the costs of having sub-stores in terms of space, equipment, personnel, and the capital tied up in stocks could far outweigh the benefits.

j) *Monitoring the environment*

The environment in which the firm operates, e.g. social, political, economic, technological, factor markets and product markets must be carefully monitored. Monitoring the environment should assist firms in identifying

Table 15: Decentralised *v.* centralised stores and stock levels

Component Bearing 67913Z (units)	Main stores	A	B	C	D	Total	Central stores system
Maximum	250	20	30	10	10	320	300
Minimum	50	5	7	3	3	68	60
Re-order level	100	8	10	5	5	—	110

threats and opportunities and enable them to adapt to change more quickly. This early warning system could help avoid some of the losses incurred by having to dispose of obsolete stocks: early warning=early action.

k) *Operational research and statistical techniques*

If forecasting and control procedures are to be improved management need to become more familiar with operational research and statistical techniques. As pointed out earlier computer packages are available and management need to find out what such packages can do for them. This field alone provides great scope for improving materials management and reducing expensive holding costs, e.g. matching stocks and production; levels of service and the probability of a 'stockout'.

l) *Behavioural aspects*

The attitude that 'thou shalt not run out of stock' needs changing to 'thou shalt ensure that stocks are kept to an acceptable minimum'. Materials management must really begin to appreciate that they are operating in a constantly changing environment and increase the frequency with which reviews of stock levels are carried out.

m) *The role of audit*

The internal and external auditors can help to detect and prevent errors and fraud and their contribution towards satisfactory control of materials should not be ignored.

n) *Organisation*

All business functions must co-operate, co-ordinate and communicate effectively. This should ensure that control systems are more effective and avoid purchasing errors caused by poor communications.

Conclusion

Management must endeavour to improve the productivity of the capital employed. Stocks held as raw materials, work-in-progress and finished goods represent capital tied up. Why finance the purchase and holding of stocks which may not be required for several months? The reduction of stocks in terms of value and volume can assist in bringing about significant savings in holding costs, e.g. interest charges, space, manpower, capital equipment, etc. The rewards from improved materials management should not be under-estimated. The effect of inflation on stocks and the risk of a 'stockout' should not be ignored. Decision making in the real and imperfect world requires management who can see both sides of the argument and base their decisions on the relevant facts and appreciate that trade offs are inevitable.

Materials management, profitability and the construction industry

'Times are getting hard, boys, money's getting scarce', may be an old song but very true of the current business environment. The real name of the game is ROI (Return on Investment) and this is particularly important not just in the construction industry, but in any industry. It could well be the case that UK industry has become so pre-occupied with labour productivity that it has tended to ignore the productivity of the capital employed. If firms are to survive the long term they cannot afford to neglect the productivity of capital. It has been said that business is all about borrowing money with one hand, putting it to work, and earning a return higher than the cost of borrowing it. Would you borrow money, at say 15 per cent, and invest it at 8 per cent? Certainly not! Investors be they individuals, companies or institutions all want a satisfactory return on their investment.

The cost profile of the construction industry (Table 16) indicates just how important materials costs are to the industry. Materials management is one area in which substantial savings could be made and profitability increased (Table 17 and Table 18). A small percentage cut in materials costs could bring about a sizeable increase in profits.

Thus, a 2 per cent cut in materials costs could increase profits by 14.6 per cent, almost double what could be achieved by a 2 per cent cut in labour costs and four times the increase which could accrue if overheads were cut by 2 per cent.

Table 16: Cost profile of the construction industry

	Materials costs %	Labour costs %	Overheads costs %	Profit %
Construction industry	51	29	13	7

Table 17: Effect on profits of cutting costs

	Materials costs % increase in profit		Labour costs % increase in profit		Overheads % increase in profit	
	2% cut	5% cut	2% cut	5% cut	2% cut	5% cut
Construction industry	14.6	36.4	8.3	20.7	3.7	9.3

Table 18: Cost reduction required to increase return on capital employed by 10 per cent

	Return on capital employed	Percentage reduction required		
		Materials costs	Labour costs	Overheads
Construction industry	% 18.3*	% 7.51	% 13.21	% 29.46

*Source: Industrial Performance Analysis, Sixth Edition 1981 (Inter Company Comparisons Ltd) – uses 1978/79 figures.

A more extreme example is given in Table 18 which answers the question: by how much must costs be reduced to increase the return on capital employed by 10 per cent?

The data highlight the need for improvements within the construction industry by materials management; improvements to cut the costs of materials used and also improvements in the control of stocks held. Reduce the volume/value of stocks held as raw materials, work-in-progress, etc. and you also reduce expensive holding costs, e.g. interest charges, purchasing costs, insurance, storage space, etc. (at the end of 1978 the stocks of materials, fuel, work-in-progress and finished goods held by UK industry amounted to a staggering £55 billion).[2]

The control of labour and overheads cannot and should not be ignored, but what can be done to cut those materials costs? More efficient materials management in the construction industry can pay dividends.

References
[1]*Cost/Profit Structure of British Industry*, Management Today, October 1977.
[2]*Stockbuilding: recent trends and prospects*, Economic Progress Report, The Treasury, June 1980, HMSO.

Mail order profitability

In today's diverse, complex and unsettled business environment, mail order companies are beginning to feel the pinch. This important sector accounts for around 10 per cent of total consumer expenditure in the range of merchandise offered.* In addition to Great Universal Stores and Littlewoods, who between them possess a 62 per cent market share, there are three other companies which together account for a further 30 per cent share of the mail order market. They are Empire Stores (Bradford) Ltd (8 per cent); Freemans (London) Ltd (12 per cent); Grattan Warehouses Ltd (12 per cent): (Source: *Retail Business*, January/April/October 1980).

These three companies could be described as being 'self-contained mail-order operators.' They have a common year end, are of a similar size and have adopted similar trading methods. A study of these three companies therefore provides a unique, interesting and valid comparison.

Have their management gone overboard in their quest for increased sales? Sales growth can on occasions lead to lower profits! Table 19 compares performance in terms of sales and profitability.

Affected by recession

The portrait painted by the above comparative performance analysis indicates quite clearly that all three companies have been affected by the current recession and have had to trim their margins. Over the past five years Free-

*Central Statistical Office, *National Income & Expenditure*, HMSO, 1980.

109

Table 19: Comparative performance

		Empire	Freemans	Grattan
SALES (£000)				
Year ended	31.1.77	76 705	130 644	137 517
	31.1.78	93 014	154 839	154 739
	31.1.79	108 806	186 016	175 602
	31.1.80	132 507	208 457	213 432*
	3 1.1.81	142 548	229 434	199 534
PROFITS (£000) (Pre-tax Profits)				
Year Ended	31.1.77	4 708	10 345	11 428
	31.1.78	6 557	13 060	11 764
	31.1.79	7 683	16 747	10 652
	31.1.80	7 382	15 521	2 367
	31.1.81	5 605	10 644	3 112
PROFITS % OF SALES				
Year ended	31.1.77	6.1	7.9	8.3
	31.1.78	7.0	8.4	7.6
	31.1.79	7.1	9.0	6.1
	31.1.80	5.6	7.4	1.1
	31.1.81	3.9	4.6	1.6
PROFITS % OF NET WORTH (Return on Investment)				
Year Ended	31.1.77	27.0	27.8	27.5
	31.1.78	26.2	29.4	26.2
	31.1.79	27.6	32.1	21.7
	31.1.80	25.1	24.9	4.7
	31.1.81	16.8	15.7	6.1

*Figure adjusted to ensure a fair comparison

Source: Published Accounts

mans has performed better than the other two. Empire has experienced steady progress and Grattan, it would appear, has problems.

The real name of the game of business is ROI (Return on Investment); management need to devote more time to improving the productivity of capital employment. In the fight to increase profitability, management may have devoted a vast amount of time and effort into reducing labour costs. Is this the answer?

Labour costs should certainly not be ignored, but there is a real danger that management may become so preoccupied with labour productivity that the areas of materials costs and overhead costs may be neglected. Table 20 indicates just how important materials and overhead costs are to the three companies.

Obviously it would be useful to have a breakdown in percentage terms of material costs and overhead costs, but such information cannot be extracted from published accounts. However, it follows that a small percentage

Table 20: The cost-profit structure 1976–1981

(% of sales value)	Empire %	Freemans %	Grattan %
Materials and overhead costs	86.48	84.77	86.17
Labour costs	7.75	7.93	9.37
Profit	5.77	7.30	4.46
	100.00	100.00	100.00

Figures above are average figures for the five years ended 31.1.81

Source: Published Accounts

Table 21: Effects on profits of cutting costs

(% increase in profits)	Empire %	Freemans %	Grattan %
2% cut in materials and overhead costs	29.98	23.22	38.64
2% cut in labour costs	2.69	2.17	4.20

decrease in the materials and overhead costs area could significantly increase profits (Table 21).

It can be observed that with a mere 2 per cent cut in materials and overhead costs profits would increase dramatically in the case of each of the companies studied, over nine times what could be achieved by a similar reduction in labour costs.

What can be done?

An effort should be made to reduce the materials costs of the products by, for instance, securing better discounts from suppliers. Inventory control in the mail order business has to be good but must be improved and can be improved (Table 22).

Stocks represent vast sums of capital tied up and also involve the companies in paying out substantial holding costs in such areas as interest

Table 22: Inventory comparison

	Empire	Freemans	Grattan
Number of days sales in stock (Average 5 years to 1.1.81)	39.4	54.2	64.6

charges, storage and insurance. Stock levels must be reduced to an acceptable minimum, however the possibility of a 'stockout' should not be overlooked.

If the companies are to survive and prosper in the future, it is essential that all management, purchasing, marketing, data processing and finance functions co-ordinate, co-operate and communicate effectively.

The purpose of this article is to highlight the problems; to solve them is not just a challenge for management but also another story.

Credit control – Mail order: a risky return

Business decisions can be regarded as a trade off between risk and return. This business dilemma is quite evident in the decision whether to allow sales on credit.

The problem of credit control is particularly acute for catalogue mail order companies because of their large numbers of agents and customers (Freemans and Grattan each have in excess of 500 000 agents and 2 500 000 customers).

In addition they send goods out on approval to their customers, and make around 90 per cent of their sales on credit.

In many business organisations the purpose of credit control ensures that there is an adequate in-flow of cash, debtors meet their obligations, and bad debts are kept to a minimum

In practice this often leads to aged lists of debtors being produced for review, and unless this procedure is handled with care there can be an over-concentration on bad debts, with slow paying accounts receiving less attention than they deserve.

Slow paying accounts merit regular attention for as H. N. Woodward* says, 'Often your most important source of finance is hidden in your balance sheet, and debtors may be the quickest source of finance'.

The sales and debtor positions for the two largest independent mail order houses, Freemans and Grattan, are shown in Table 23. The table shows the increasing difficulty in collecting cash from debtors as the recession deepened in the year to 31 January 1981.

Average debtors as a percentage of sales have increased for both Freemans and Grattan.

If the two companies had been able to operate at the level of debtors to sales achieved in the best of the last five years, the reduction in average debt would have been as shown in Table 24.

The calculation of savings does not imply that the best year within the last five was the best which could be achieved and there could, therefore, be even greater potential savings.

There are several ways of chasing outstanding accounts including: the use of Pareto Analysis in identifying problem accounts; a system of reminder letters, e.g. sent via computer; use of the telephone for personal contact

*Woodward, H. N., *Management Strategies for Small Companies*, Harvard Business Review Jan/Feb 1976.

Table 23: Comparison of Sales and Debtors

	Freemans		Grattan	
	£000	percentage plus	£000	percentage plus
Sales including VAT				
Year ended 31.1.77	140.611		148.518	
31.1.78	166.474	18.4	166.685	12.2
31.1.79	200.232	20.3	189.237	13.5
31.1.80	231.248	15.5	239.616	26.6
31.1.81	260.127	12.5	227.129	−5.2
Debtors including VAT				
Year ended 31.1.76	35.850		36.349	
31.1.77	39.448	10.0	42.597	17.2
31.1.78	46.306	17.4	45.963	7.9
31.1.79	55.481	19.8	54.837	19.3
31.1.80	67.440	21.6	70.742	29.0
31.1.81	75.235	11.6	60.450	−14.5
Average debtors as a percentage of sales	%		%	
Year to 31.1.77	26.8		26.6	
31.1.78	25.8		26.6	
31.1.79	25.4		26.6	
31.1.80	26.6		26.2	
31.1.81	27.4		28.9	

Source: Company Accounts

Table 24: Savings from a reduction in Debtors

	Freemans	Grattan
	£000	£000
Sales year to 31.1.81	260 127	227 129
% reduction of debt to sales	27.4%−25.4% = 2%	28.9%−26.2% = 2.7%
	£000	£000
Amount of potential debtors reduction	5 202	6 132
Potential cost saving at 15% Finance Cost	780	920

(approximately 70 per cent of households now have a telephone); personal visits; and employment of debt collection specialists.

All these techniques are used to a greater or lesser extent by the catalogue mail order companies.

The real danger is that the costs of reminder activities are easily seen, but the benefits are less easy to quantify.

This may lead to a cost-cutting exercise, when cash flow problems exist and profits are under pressure, when really credit control needs to be strengthened.

The mail order companies are competing with other demands on the household budget and the organisation with the weakest credit control system is likely to be the last in the queue for payment – it may acquire a reputation of being a 'soft touch'.

As stated at the outset, business decisions balance risk against return. The appointment of mail order agents is a prime example of this principle in that the potential for doing profitable business is measured against the prospects of incurring bad debts.

The mail order companies have applied the techniques of management science to the appointment process. By applying the theory of normal distribution and probability to various demographic characteristics, a credit rating can be produced for each applicant.

Once appointed, the mail order agent's activity is controlled by the use of a credit limit, suspension of deliveries in the event of credit limits being reached, or other predetermined circumstances, and the use of the techniques for collecting outstanding debts outlined above.

It could well be the case that catalogue mail order companies have gone overboard on improving their systems for order processing and prompt delivery of merchandise. Agreed, this aspect of a mail order company's business is important, but could the improvements introduced be at the expense of neglecting to improve credit control?

Debt collection times are extending in most business sectors. Never has it been more important for companies to examine their credit control procedures for completeness and effectiveness in aiming at the correct balance between risk and return.

 Devising a sound creditor policy

Nowadays managements assign a high priority to the credit-control system, the purpose of such a system being to ensure that debtors pay up within a reasonable period of time and to avoid bad debts. Yes, businesses of all shapes and sizes do, in fact, spend a lot of time and effort on shaping their credit policy! Sadly, however, businesses tend to neglect a *creditor* policy! Creditors provide a vast amount of short-term finance, so management should therefore devote more time to devising a sound creditor policy.

Since trade creditors arise from the purchasing department, this places purchasing – and the operating cycle which follows the receipt of goods – in the forefront of cost control. It must be remembered that purchasing cuts across functional barriers and that its activities tend to reflect the increasingly competitive nature of business.

Effective cash management results from a flexible yet pre-determined policy for all current assets and current liabilities. There is a wealth of literature on the management of debtors and inventory control as a means to achieving the objectives of such a policy, but surprisingly little attention has been devoted to the need for a policy on the management of current liabilities. For the purpose of this article, as it relates to working capital management and cashflow, 'current liabilities' are taken to mean trade creditors and accruals.

An integrated aproach to cash management through the working cycle must ensure that the velocity of cash outflows match the speed with which money is recovered from debtors. The number of days that creditors remain outstanding can have a fundamental impact on cashflows in the way that the ratio of debtor days outstanding can ease or exacerbate company liquidity. Warnes[1] makes the point when he states that 'creditors should be treated similarly to debtors, by establishing a limit of acceptable creditor days beyond which non-payment to suppliers indicates financial danger'.

Gibbs[2] believes the key to a creditor policy is 'consistency'. He argues that a company which is habitually a slow but reliable payer will not unduly alarm the seller. To counteract the extension of credit granted to the buyer, the seller may, however, increase the price of the goods. Clearly the buyer must guard against this form of interest charge by keeping abreast of competitors' prices.

There are other constraints, apart from price rises and discounts that may deter a buyer from taking excessive credit, including the following:

- Deterioration in service to compensate the supplier for the slow payment of his bills.
- Possible disruption of the business if creditors cut off supplies.
- Inability to obtain new sources of supply due to the company's poor credit rating.
- Fear of putting suppliers out of business due to the shortage of cash.
- Increased administration costs of dealing with telephone calls, letters and statements in respect of overdue accounts.

A company's creditor policy is shaped to a great extent by the structure of the industry. In certain cases a specific industry sets the actual credit terms. Credit terms will be subject to the relative bargaining power of both the supplier and the buyer. This relationship, according to Porter,[3] forms two of the five competitive forces which determine industry profitability. A buyer is in a powerful position where the following conditions apply:

- Purchases are concentrated or in large volume, especially if the seller has high fixed costs.
- The products are undifferentiated.
- The buyer poses a significant threat in terms of backward vertical integration.

- The purchase is a significant fraction of the product cost.
- The buyer's custom is a significant part of the seller's turnover.

In devising a policy on creditors the power relationships between buyer and seller should not be overlooked. For some companies this relationship alone may well be the factor which ultimately shapes their policy.

Two other factors also play a role in determining a company's policy on creditors and these will now be briefly discussed.

For many companies, especially small companies, trade credit is a very useful and necessary form of short-term finance. Indeed, Smith[4] argues that 'accounts payable ... represents a large portion of short-term financing'. According to Boyle,[5] trade credit can be as much as 60 per cent of the current liabilities for non-financial firms and this percentage is often somewhat larger for small firms because they may not qualify for finance from other sources. Through necessity, they rely rather heavily on trade credit.

One of the benefits of using trade credit as a source of finance is that it is 'spontaneous', arising from ordinary business transactions. It therefore adjusts naturally to the level of business activity. If, for example, a firm makes normal purchases of £2000 per day on 30 days' credit, on average it will owe 30 times £2000 or £60 000 to its suppliers. This is clearly an attractive proposition for a firm that has strictly limited borrowing opportunities.

The importance of accounts payable as a source of corporate finance is not confined to small companies. Table 25 summarises the manner in which ICI funded its multinational operations at its financial year-end 31 December 1982. It is often overlooked that supplier finance does have a cost, not least an opportunity cost, e.g. using the cash for capital equipment or other investments.

The final factor to which a creditor policy must address itself is the question of settlement discounts, since it is important for a company to weigh the advantages of delayed payments to creditors against the benefits that accrue from prompt payment and the availability of settlement discounts. Quite

Table 25: Extract from ICI Report 1982

Short term	£m	£m
Creditors	1386	
Short-term borrowing	531	1917
Long term		
Grants and deferred liabilities	426	
Loans	1536	
Capital and reserves	3417	5379
		7296

Source: *Journal of General Management*, Vol. 9, No. 4, Summer 1984.

Table 26: An example of settlement discount

Invoice value	£10 000
Supplier's normal credit terms	30 days following invoice date
Early payment $2\frac{1}{2}$ per cent discount	7 days following invoice date
Marginal administration cost	£20
Bank overdraft cost	15 per cent p.a.
Value of normal credit period	$= \dfrac{30}{365} \times \dfrac{15}{100} \times £10\,000$
	$= £123$
Value of early payment credit period	$= \left[\left(\dfrac{7}{365} \times \dfrac{15}{100} \right) (£10\,000) + (2.5\% \text{ of } £10\,000) \right] - 20$
	$= £259$
Therefore the net cash saved by taking cash discount	$= £259 - £123$
	$= £136$

apart from any financial gain or loss there is the question of supplier goodwill to consider – and one's credit rating!

It has been established that the annualised cost of settlement discount can be as high as 30 to 40 per cent and therefore it may well be profitable for a company to increase its overdraft (if this is possible) in order to avail itself of settlement discount. In the context of this discussion it is probably more meaningful if the question of settlement discounts is examined by reference to an example (see Table 26).

Management of accruals 獲利

Accruals can be thought of mainly as the operating expenses of the business and include such items as wages, salaries, tax, national insurance and VAT. In common with trade creditors they provide a spontaneous source of credit helping to finance working capital. Unlike trade creditors, however, management is relatively constrained in terms of what can be done to influence accruals for cash management purposes.

However, the short-term financing resulting from accrued wages and/or salaries can be considerable. During the last ten to 15 years many companies have changed their wages and salaries payment procedures from weekly to monthly. The stated reason of 'administrative convenience' may well have been the driving force behind the change of procedures, but the fact remains that employees are providing employers with an interest-free loan!

Employers also derive considerable benefit from the weekly or monthly deductions of national insurance and income tax from employees' remuneration. This money is paid in arrears and remains in the company's bank account until the monthly returns are made to the Inland Revenue, thus effectively reducing the interest charges on the company's bank account.

Normally, the returns are due on the fifth of the month, but 14 days' grace is allowed so, in effect, the payment can be delayed until the nineteenth of the month.

Further savings can be made by delaying the transfer of funds to the Revenue, although overdue tax does incur a liability to interest calculated from when the tax falls due to the date of payment.

It is often stated that a company operates as an unpaid tax-collector since most companies must collect PAYE, ACT and submit VAT at regular intervals. For many companies, VAT collection, together with the necessary paperwork, is an onerous task but it does provide a company with the use of funds from the moment an account is settled until the time the VAT is submitted to the Customs and Excise.

Normal practice dictates that VAT is forwarded every three months, so on average a company has 45 days' interest-free credit. For a company due to submit £100 000 with a cost of capital of 10 per cent, this form of financing is worth £1250:

$$£100\,000 \times 10\% \times \frac{45}{360} = £1250$$

If beset by a liquidity (i.e. cashflow) crisis, a company should prepare a schedule of priority payments and thought should be directed towards preferential creditors such as the Revenue, Customs and interest due to the bank on the company overdraft. A further financial commitment may result from interim or final dividend to shareholders, for it is important in terms of the company image to ensure that dividends are paid.

Conclusions

It has been established that a policy should be carefully considered in relation to creditors, as is the case for debtors. Those responsible for introducing the policy must take account of a range of factors which include consistency of policy, constraints imposed by the supplier in response to slow payers, the power relationships that exist between buyer and seller and the financial implications of taking settlement discount.

Since creditors are the direct result of the purchasing function, the purchasing department can contribute to effective working capital management.

An informed and consistent policy on creditors and accruals does not appear to have received the attention it deserves for it has much to offer towards an integrated approach to cash management.

References
[1]Warnes, B., 'Control accounting', *Accountancy Age*, May 1984.
[2]Gibbs, J., *A Practical Approach to Financial Management* (Financial Training Publications, 1978).
[3]Porter, M. E., *Competitive Advantage* (Collier Macmillan, 1985).
[4]Smith, K. V., *Guide to Working Capital* (McGraw Hill, 1979).
[5]Boyle, J., *Managerial Finance* (Holt, Rinehart and Winston, 1979).

Buried treasure: Internal sources of finance – the management and control of Fixed Assets and Working Capital

Treasure! Where?

Management tend to seek new funds instead of making better use of those which they already have.[1] A firm's Balance Sheet is rather like a treasure map, in that it frequently contains hidden capital, because the management and control of Fixed Assets and Working Capital has been neglected. Finance is an extremely scarce and expensive commodity and should be used in exactly the same way as any other factor of production, that is, with efficiency. It is of utmost importance that management are actively involved and concerned with cash flow and the productivity of capital.[2] Efficient management and control of Fixed Assets and Working Capital can help to generate a considerable amount of finance.

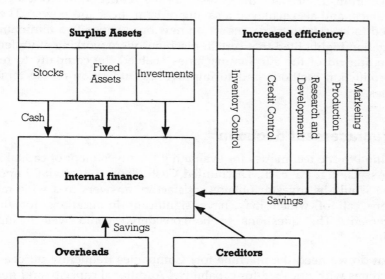

Fig. 4.6 *Internal finance from Fixed Assets and Working Capital*

So where are all these sources of finance which are hidden in the Balance Sheet?

Surplus assets

A strategy of surplus asset recognition and disposal is quite likely to: make a substantial improvement in cash flow; reduce overheads; increase the space available for production, storage of inventory and administration; improve machine utilisation. Fixed Assets and Current Assets, such as stock, represent capital tied up in physical resources. If these resources are not being used, the productivity of capital is bound to suffer. In addition to this they are also tying up funds which could be used elsewhere in the organisation.

Case study

Following a very careful review of all their business assets Wik Ltd discovered that certain machines, office equipment and inventory items were surplus to requirements. Buyers were found (finding a buyer does create a problem and should not be under-estimated) and the sale of the surplus assets realised £29 250 (cash flow improved, at a stroke). The space vacated by the sale of certain fixed assets was used for further company expansion (expanding without having to provide a new building). However, if the company had not needed the additional space created, it may have been possible to sell or sub-let all/some of it which would also bring about a reduction in overheads such as rates, insurance and holding costs. The company did in fact experience a reduction in insurance as a direct result of the reduction in stock levels and plant values, and also achieved a saving of light, heat and power. They also managed to keep interest payments on new borrowings to a minimum. The investigation highlighted that certain machines were working at under-capacity. Getting rid of the surplus machines enabled the company to re-think their production methods and to improve the utilisation of the remaining machines.

The replacement decision

In addition to the techniques for evaluating the investment of capital in new Fixed Assets, e.g. Payback, Discounted Cash Flow, it is of vital importance that the would-be investor obtains satisfactory answers to a wide range of questions, all of which may have significant implications for financial management. The questions to be considered could well include the following:

a) What do we need the machine for? Companies frequently purchase new machines with uncalled-for capability.[3] Additional capacity and flexibility which may never ever be used ties up finance unnecessarily.
b) Will the supplier be prepared to allow a trade in allowance on the old Fixed Asset? 'Ask and ye shall find out.' The allowance could be much greater than the asset's scrap value.
c) Are there any competent sub-contractors? If so, the company's investment in Fixed Assets and inventory could be drastically reduced, not to mention the savings in overheads.
d) Is it possible to lease or hire the Fixed Asset? This would free the company from having to find an extremely large lump sum and could be regarded as 'a hedge against obsolescence'. Disposing of an obsolete Fixed Asset is not an easy task and could well result in a substantial loss. It could certainly

prove much easier to cancel, complete or re-arrange a contract for the hire of an asset.

e) What is the opportunity cost? (i.e. the alternative foregone.)

The replacement decision also involves consideration of a multitude of non-financial factors such as: availability of spares, frequency of maintenance, quality of after-sales service, standardisation of Fixed Assets, delivery, reliability. However, all of these non-financial factors could well affect a firm's financial performance at some future date. Lost production would occur if a machine was out of use because of a breakdown or non-availability of spares. Standardisation of Fixed Assets would reduce the need to significantly increase the stocks of spare parts, avoid the costs involved in re-training operatives, and ensure that the costs of routine maintenance are not permitted to escalate.

Inventory control

Stocks represent capital tied up in goods, therefore if stock levels can be reduced, the amount of capital can also be reduced. In addition to savings in interest payments and the freeing of storage space the holding costs (e.g. storage, handling and re-handling, insurance) should be reduced. Reducing stock levels also lessens the risk of loss caused by obsolescence or deterioration.

Inventories of raw materials, work-in-progress and finished goods, do for many firms represent a substantial investment. A small percentage reduction in inventory levels could, therefore, be responsible for savings amounting to several thousand pounds. It must be remembered that there is a trade off between reducing stocks and the risk of causing production to come to a halt because of a 'stockout'.

What can inventory management do?

a) Management must review maximum, minimum and re-order stock levels at regular intervals and take seasonal fluctuations into account. This necessitates very close co-operation and co-ordination between all business functions, e.g. Finance, Production, Marketing. There is a great temptation on the part of the store-keepers to maintain high stocks in order to avoid production hold ups.

b) *Pareto Analysis*[4] has been successful in improving inventory control and could prove to be a worthwhile exercise. 'Twenty per cent of your stock, could account for 80 per cent of your total inventory value'. Careful control of the 20 per cent, therefore implies that a vast proportion of the total stock valuation is subjected to greater scrutiny.

c) Firms have been known to order stock from suppliers which they could have obtained from within their own stores. This situation highlights the fact that a firm really does need a satisfactory *material classification system*.[5] Such a system should be capable of ascertaining whether particular items exist, and their location.

d) *The regular delivery system*[6] is worthy of consideration. Suppliers deliver components/materials at frequent intervals, which within a very short space of time are converted into finished goods and despatched to customers. This system can dramatically reduce a company's holding costs.

Credit control

The frequency with which cash flows into the firm from debtors and the avoidance of bad debts, in brief sums up what credit control is all about. The usual methods of credit control involve: credit screening, credit limits, aged analysis of debtors, systems of letters to slow payers, suspension of deliveries and discounts for prompt payment. However, it may be possible to achieve more effective credit control by:

a) *Telephone contact.* A single telephone call may quickly establish the reason why a particular debtor has not paid. The reason for non-payment could well be the supplier's own fault, e.g. relevant supplier's staff were not informed that the wrong quality was delivered to a customer because of a poor communication system.

b) *Involving sales executives* in the credit control process. Remember that salesmen actually talk to customers at frequent intervals and may be able to provide valuable information.

c) *A penalty for introducing bad debts.* It is no use making a sale if you do not get paid. It would at least make sales people more careful about who they sell to. Sales could however fall, if sales people became over-cautious in accepting new business.

d) *Recognition of customers' payment systems.* This would ensure that documentation such as invoices and statements arrive in time to obtain payment as early as practicable.

e) *Employ a debt collection specialist*, e.g. to collect debt from Hire Purchase debtors.

f) *Contra.* It may be possible to buy something on credit from your debtor and simply offset the debt.

Improvement in credit control can certainly improve a firm's cash flow position within a relatively short space of time.

Retained profits

If companies are to survive and grow, a large plough-back is essential. Retained profits comprise one of the principal sources of company finance in the UK. Efficient use of fixed assets, improved inventory control, effective credit control and careful co-ordination of business functions can improve profitability and enable an even greater ploughback. It is therefore possible for a firm to produce more finance from internal sources simply by becoming more efficient in the ways in which it organises, manages, operates and controls the scarce resources at its disposal.

Finance from creditors

The time lag between the delivery of goods and the payment of suppliers provides short-term finance, e.g. three months. However, if discounts are offered in return for prompt payment, it could certainly be to a firm's advantage to pay promptly. The discount rate offered, although small, could in fact have a substantial effective annual rate of interest in excess of 20 per cent. It must also be remembered that if firms place too much reliance upon finance from creditors this could cause their liquidity position to deteriorate.

Audit

The role of internal and external audit in the control and management of Fixed Assets and Working Capital should not be underestimated. It is the responsibility of management to ensure that adequate systems of internal control are in operation. It is the task of the auditors to assess the efficiency of those systems and to inform management of any possible weaknesses. In this way losses due to errors and fraud may be minimised.

The Banker's role – advising firms

Numerous reports and articles have over the years pointed to an 'information gap' as being responsible for firms having difficulty in obtaining finance from external sources. This obsession with the problems of raising funds from external sources, although very important, has in my view been at the expense of making firms more aware of their internal sources of capital. Firms not only need advice upon how to obtain finance but also need to know how to make the best possible use of it. It could well be the case, that nowadays there is such a wealth of information available that the real problem is a 'communication gap'. Thus, there is a great need for bankers to provide advice and communicate relevant information relating to both internal and external financing.[7] Bankers are in a prime position to develop this ancillary advice service to meet the needs of their customers and to bridge the 'communication gap'. Banks have been instrumental in stimulating more interest in the use of Budgetary Control simply by requiring firms to produce cash flow forecasts in support of an application for an advance. Assistance given now to encourage firms to make better use of the finance which they already employ can only prove to promote the banks' long-term success. If your banking customer can: first of all survive, secondly develop and grow, thirdly become more efficient and lastly be managed more effectively, then the bank will also grow and prosper.

Conclusion

Management must strive to make better use of the funds which they already possess. ROI (Return on Investment) is the real name of the game. An investment should yield an adequate return, for every investment has an opportunity cost. The productivity of capital and concern with cash flow are both areas of utmost importance. 'Buried Treasure' can be found in the form of surplus assets, the type of replacement decision, more effective inventory control, more efficient credit control and improving business efficiency, all of which may either increase cash flow and/or ensure more profits are available for retention.

Bankers are in the front line when it comes to the provision of advice and communication of relevant business/financial information. Banks may, by helping firms improve their performance, secure their own long-term future.

The banker as a business adviser, can make a most worthwhile contribution towards the recovery of British industry, in tomorrow's complex and diverse business environment.

References

[1]Chadwick, L., 'Should We Be More Inward Looking – For That Extra Finance;, *Management Accounting*, February 1980.
[2]Woodward, H.N., 'Management Strategies For Small Companies', *Certified Accountant*, August 1976.
[3]Lockyer, Prof. K.G., 'Factory and Production Management', Pitman.
[4]Zimmerman, G.W., 'The ABCs of Vilfredo Pareto', *Production & Inventory Management*, September 1975.
[5]Brisch, E.G., 'Maximum Ex Minimo', June 1954.
[6]Chadwick, L., 'The History of Holset Engineering 1952–1977', MBA Dissertation, University of Bradford 1977.
[7]Back, R.D., 'The Branch Manager As An Adviser To Small Firms', *Journal of the Institute of Bankers*, December 1977.

Generation of internal finance by production management

Production management will always be particularly concerned with the productivity of their company; however, they should also be concerned with a different type of productivity – **the productivity of capital employed**.

The production area in many firms employs a very significant concentration of finance. As finance is an extremely expensive and scarce resource, production management must ensure by their decisions and actions that it is used efficiently. It is, therefore, of paramount importance that there is close co-operation and co-ordination between all the functions of the business, e.g. Fig. 4.7.

Production management should be vigorously involved in both aspects of the generation of internal finance (Fig. 4.8). Their contribution towards retained earnings is seldom in dispute, but what they must really strive for, is to *make better use of the finance that has already been invested in their company*.

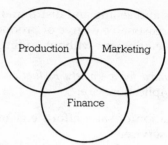

Fig. 4.7 *Functional inter-dependence*

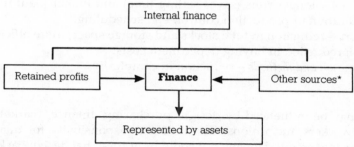

Fig. 4.8 *Internal finance*

How can production management help to manufacture finance from internal sources?

There are numerous ways in which production management can help make better use of the finance that a firm is already using, both at the product design stage and during manufacture.

The product

Variety

Variety may be described as 'the spice of life', but variety in relation to production tends to *increase complexity and causes costs to escalate*. An increase in variety is quite likely to cause organisational problems. It is almost certain that Production Planning and Control will become more time-consuming as scheduling and machine loading problems tend to multiply. Variety can also be very costly when it comes to product design, in terms of man hours expended and equipment required. It is argued that variety will substantially increase the amount of capital tied up in inventory, factory space, administration and manufacturing equipment.[1] 'Variety of your products could force you to stock a larger variety of components and lead you to employ a larger variety of men (skills) and machines'. This also implies a dramatic increase in overheads such as holding costs, rent and rates, insurance, running costs,

*The finance which the firm already possesses, e.g. invested in Fixed Assets and Working Capital.

125

buying department costs and selling and distribution costs. However, it may be possible to achieve a reasonable degree of product variety by standardisation of components and equipment without adding too much to complexity and costs.

Some of the benefits claimed for a Variety Reduction Programme,[1] all of which have marked financial implications are:

a) *Marketing* – intensification of sales effort, e.g. more effective advertising and better after-sales service.
b) *Design* – greater design productivity and a better understanding of the design problems which occur.
c) *Production* – longer runs (saves setting time) and higher plant utilisation. Simplification of production control, e.g. scheduling.
d) *Inventory* – reduction in total stocks and storage space; more efficient stock control; reduction in buying department costs.
e) *Organisation and methods* – reduction in complexity.

Quality

Quality may be influenced by design, purchasing, finance, marketing, production, workers and unions. The ultimate responsibility for quality rests with top management. However, it could be argued that design backed up by efficient quality control is of prime importance. Design, to ensure that the product fulfils the function for which it is required and meets the needs of the consumers, should also *eliminate uncalled for quality*, e.g. where the product is fit for the purpose for which it is designed using less expensive materials such as plastic in place of brass and performance remains unimpaired. It is becoming increasingly evident that quality control cannot be regarded as a separate function, completely independent of the design, manufacturing and marketing activities of an organisation.[2] In addition to sampling techniques, control charts and inspection methods with which quality control is frequently associated the relationship between product quality, process control, maintenance and after-sales service must also form part of the total quality concept.

Cost savings can therefore be made by eliminating uncalled for quality in design, in the product and in production.

Management must also attempt to *cut out uncalled for precision*. As precision increases, e.g. machining a casting to a very fine tolerance, costs increase. What a waste if an inch either way would not make any difference to the performance of the product.

Value analysis

Value analysis is a *cost reduction and control technique* which operates by attacking the basic design of the product to ascertain inefficiency by analysis of function (function – 'that property of the product which makes it sell'). The procedure involves answering certain key questions such as:

a) What is the product's function? (What does it do?)
b) How else can this function be achieved? (What are the alternatives?)

c) How many components are needed? (Are they *all* necessary?)

d) What is the cost of each alternative course of action? (How much?)

Manufacture

Classification system

Why order materials which are already in your stores from outside suppliers? This could well be the case where the firm does not employ an efficient materials classification system. The classification system must[3]:

a) Make it possible to find an existing item.

b) Ascertain whether or not a particular item exists.

c) Find all items capable of satisfying a given need.

d) Find all the needs which a given item can satisfy.

e) Ensure that there is one place, and one place only, for all existing items and future additions.

What is wrong with British industry?

- Unwilling to invest in new machinery?
- Bad management?
- Unfair competition from overseas?
- Trade unions?
- Poor industrial relations?
- Slow to develop new technology?
- Taxation?
- Legislation?

It can be observed from Table 27 that considerable savings may be obtained by *more efficient utilisation of men and machines*. The Midlands Tomorrow survey highlighted the fact that one of British industry's major problems is not necessarily a shortage of investment in plant and machinery, but one of utilising more fully its existing manufacturing fixed assets. Industry, therefore, needs to make better use of the capital which has already been invested in plant and machinery. British industry really needs to invest in *organisation*[5] – improved plant lay-out, better production planning and control, more effective material handling, work and method study leading to a reduction in waiting and idle time.

Work study

Work study is not just concerned with the age old problem of how long it should take one operative to perform a particular operation. It is also concerned with operating methods, selection of equipment, usage of equipment, lay-out, supply and usage of materials, availability of ancillary services. All of which are areas in which *finance can be saved simply by becoming more efficient*.

Table 27: Utilisation of Labour and Machinery

Utilisation of labour

Industry	Operating %	Attending %	Handling %	Servicing %	Waiting management responsible %	Waiting operative responsible %
Iron and steel	43	8	24	4.5	10.5	10
Electrical	50	6	23	4.5	5	11.5
Non-ferrous	45	16	18.5	5	6	9.5
Motor vehicle components	55	10	15.5	4.5	4.5	10.5

Utilisation of machines

Industry	Productive %	Setting %	Tool adjustment %	Maintenance %	Idle time management responsible %	Idle time operative responsible %
Iron and steel	42	7.5	3.5	3.5	36	7.5
Electrical	30	4	1.5	1	59	4.5
Non-ferrous	45	2.5	1	3	44	3.5
Motor vehicle components	45	3	2.5	1.5	41	7

Source: Midlands Tomorrow survey[4]

Ergonomics

The study of man in his working environment is known in the UK as ergonomics and as human engineering in the USA.

Man is a variable, thus equipment should be capable of rapid adjustment. All too often man's physical requirements are ignored resulting in stress and discomfort. This of course is bound to affect productivity, e.g. lost production and an increase in defectives. Management must ensure that man's physical environment, e.g. lighting, climate, layout of controls and man's psychological needs are carefully considered and assist to *improve productivity*.

Conclusion

Production management can make very significant improvements in the productivity of capital. A programme of variety reduction and the elimination of uncalled for quality and precision can enable a firm to make much better use of the capital that it has already invested, thus freeing finance for other purposes. There are many questions posed by value analysis which need to be answered at the outset, during the design stage. Care and thought at the design stage may save thousands of pounds later on.

Investment in new plant and machinery may not necessarily provide the answer to the problems of British industry. In fact many firms may suffer from an overcapacity. What is really needed is an investment in the organisation of:

- Design – products and production systems
- Resources
- Production Planning and Control (including Scheduling)
- Work and Method Study
- Factory lay-out
- Material Handling, Storage and Control
- The Working Environment
- Co-ordination between functions

Only then will production management be able to make inroads into increasing labour and machine utilisation and *produce finance in addition to products*.

References
[1]Lockyer, Prof. K. G., 'Factory and Production Management' (Pitman).
[2]Elion, S. and King, J. R., 'Overall Production Control', *Management for Engineers*, Inst. of Mechanical Engineers.
[3]Brisch, E. G., 'Maximum Ex Minimo', *Inst. of Production Engineers Journal*, June 1954.
[4]West Midlands Economic Planning Council, 'Midlands Tomorrow', 1975.
[5]Edward, G. A. B., 'The Organisation of Work', SSRC Newsletter, April 1975.

The role of marketing in internal finance

In addition to the finance provided by ploughing back profits and selling off surplus assets, management may be able to generate additional finance simply by improving the efficiency of the various business functions (Fig. 4.9).

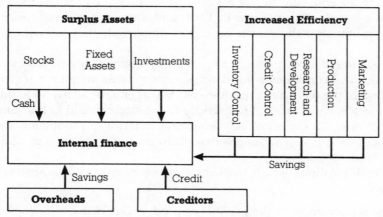

Fig. 4.9 *Internal finance from Fixed Assets and Working Capital and increased efficiency*

Comments extracted from some of the functional directors relating to the importance of their particular function could well be as follows:

Production Director: 'We are the real creators of wealth. If we don't produce it, all is lost.'

Finance Director: 'No firm can survive without adequate financial management. No finance, no business.'

Marketing Director: 'It doesn't really matter what anyone else does, if we don't sell it the firm goes bust.'

If a firm is going to bring about an increase in the productivity of capital employed, it is of paramount importance[1] that all business functions co-operate, co-ordinate and communicate effectively.

The role of marketing

Enormous sums of money are involved in areas which may be described as marketing activities, such as advertising, packaging, product development, distribution, etc. Marketing management therefore has a key part to play in ensuring that the best possible use is made of the finance which a firm already employs.

One of the mistakes made by management in the past was to see its role as producing products and selling them (sales orientation), rather than as that of meeting the *needs* of consumers (consumer orientation).[2] This one mistake has on quite a number of occasions proved very costly in terms of profits, jobs, markets, survival and the productivity of capital.

What can marketing management do to increase the productivity of capital? In brief, the answer is . . . quite a lot.

Sales growth

Many companies believe that growth in their sales figures (i.e. market share) is the 'be all and end all' for success in business. To increase sales could involve a substantial increase in fixed and variable overhead, which may reduce profits and the return on capital employed, ROI (return on investment).

All too often there is pressure from top management supported by rewards in the form of commission to increase sales volume without adequate consideration of the financial consequences. Managements also tend to introduce new products which are not only costly to develop but add to the complexity of operations. Variety is not only expensive in terms of production and stock holding costs[3] but also adds considerably to marketing costs, e.g. administration, advertising, etc.

The real questions which marketing management need to answer in this area are:

- Is the sales volume of the product or product line rising or falling?
- Is the product making a profit?

- What is the gross margin of each product?
- Does the product satisfy the customers' needs? Why not ask them?
- How is the selling price fixed? Could we be selling at a price which is too low?
- Do we offer too wide a range and too much variety?

Reducing the number of products or product lines has been found to be one of the surest routes to increased profitability.[4]

Simplification and standardisation

One of the major lessons to be learned from a study of production management is that variety is expensive. This fact is equally applicable to marketing management but is frequently overlooked. A strategy of simplification and standardisation will reduce complexity and therefore reduce costs, e.g. stock holding costs. However, it must be remembered that a reasonable amount of variety can be achieved even when using standardised components.

Credit control

The credit policy of a firm may be regarded as one of several variables which together comprise the marketing mix (the other variables are product, price, promotion, place). In addition to being actively involved in the formulation of credit policy the marketing staff have an important role to play in the area of credit control. The marketing team working in the field are in the front line when it comes to obtaining information such as:

- Why someone has not paid their account.
- Do we need to offer certain customers a cash discount?
- Should we allow a prospective customer credit or increase an existing customer's credit limit (credit screening information)?
- Is a customer in financial difficulty and likely to go into liquidation?

Marketing staff need to be made more aware that one of the objectives of credit control is to minimise bad debts. It is no use whatsoever selling goods to a customer who will never pay. Perhaps the reward system should also have a penalty in the form of a deduction from the sales bonus related to bad debts introduced. However, care would have to be taken to see that sales staff do not become over cautious.

New products

Accountants and marketing management need to work very closely when costing new products. Failure to do so could well lead to the discontinuance of reasonably profitable existing products. The reason for the discontinuance stems from the fact that some of the overheads and development costs which really apply to the new product have, because of the costing system, been absorbed by the existing products. The effect of this is to overstate profits on new products and understate profits on existing products. Thus the accounting treatment of expenditure involved in launching new products and financing research and development must be very carefully considered.

Product life cycles

It is of paramount importance that marketing management are aware of the stage that each product has reached in its life cycle. This awareness should create an atmosphere in which more time and thought are given to extending product lives and the search for new products.

The product portfolio[5] probably needs more time and effort expended on its management than does an investment portfolio. However, the aim of both portfolios is the same, namely to achieve the right mix which will optimise the return on investment and contribute towards the firm's long-term survival and prosperity.

Monitoring the environment

Marketing personnel can play a prominent part in monitoring the diverse and constantly changing environment in which the firm operates (Fig. 4.10).

Marketing staff engaged in 'on the road' duties are in constant touch with customers and encounter at first hand many of the forces which make up a firm's external environment, e.g. changes in technology, demand information, developing social pressures, why customers have switched to a competitor. They are in an ideal position to report back on the threats and the opportunities posed by changes in the external environment. The information acquired should provide considerable assistance to their firm's corporate planners and assist in ensuring that the concern is able to fulfil its objectives. It is not enough just to measure threats from competitors. It is also becoming

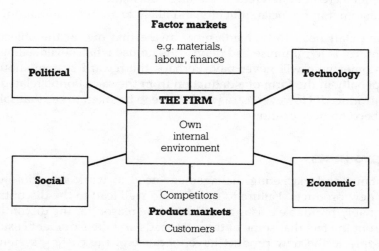

Fig. 4.10 *The business environment*

more and more necessary to monitor other industries. To ignore what is happening in other industries could prove fatal, e.g. the effect of the electronics industry on the Swiss watch industry.

Pareto's Law states that 20 per cent of your stock could account for 80 per cent of your profits.[6] True, but it also has applications which may prove useful to marketing. Management needs to identify and capitalise on their more profitable fast moving lines.

Packaging

A large proportion of the final product cost may be taken up by packaging. Marketing management are coming under increasing pressure from environmentalists who would like to see a slowing down in the diminution of the world's scarce resources. The 'throw away society' in which we live has developed and grown as a direct result of the way in which products are packaged, e.g. non-returnable bottles. Management has also a social responsibility. However, socially responsible action in relation to packaging could well save money without loss of sales. Packaging is one of the marketing variables and may not be half as critical as price. Marketing management really need to find out the answers to questions such as:

- Just how vital to the marketing mix is packaging?
- What do our competitors use?
- What else could we use?
- How would the consumer like the product to be packaged?
- Would the consumer be prepared to pay slightly less for the product to be packaged a little more simply?

Simplification of packaging (i.e. type of materials used and elimination of unnecessary materials) could also bring about savings in holding costs, overhead and interest charges, simply by tying up less capital in stocks and requiring less sophisticated packaging equipment.

Promotion

For many firms, their advertising and promotional costs form the most significant proportion of the total product cost. Here also there are questions which need to be answered if the productivity of capital is to be improved, such as:

- Which mode (e.g. TV, newspapers, etc.) is the most appropriate?
- What do our competitors use?
- Can a 10-second TV advert be as effective as a 20-second one?
- Is the advert shown when our target market is most likely to be watching? A showing at a peak viewing time could be the wrong time – why advertise to the wrong market?
- How much needs to be spent to achieve the targets set? There could well be some overspending.

There are many questions but in business there are no easy answers and numerous trade-offs, hence the need for management to assess the issues and make decisions.

Distribution

Channels of distribution need to be very carefully selected. Having your own warehouses and fleet of delivery vehicles involves a huge outlay of finance in terms of the cost of the fixed assets and associated revenue expenditure. Why organise and manage your own fleet of vehicles when there are competent sub-contractors? Repairs, maintenance and replacement of vehicles are no problem when you engage the services of a sub-contractor.

Conclusions

Marketing management have a very important role to play in ensuring that the finance which a firm already has is used efficiently and thereby increasing the productivity of capital. There are numerous questions which must be answered in relation to sales growth (growth for growth's sake), standardisation of components, credit control, the introduction of new products, product life cycles, monitoring of the business environment, Pareto, packaging, promotion and distribution.

The questions posed cannot be answered by marketing management alone. All of the business functions must work together to fight, conquer and succeed in tomorrow's diverse and complex environment.

References
[1] Chadwick, L., 'Generation of internal finance by production management', *Management Accounting*, July/August 1980.
[2] Kotier, P., *Marketing Management* (Prentice-Hall).
[3] Lockyer, K. G., *Factory and Production Management* (Pitman).
[4] Woodward, H. N., 'Management strategies for small companies', *Certified Accountant*, August 1976.
[5] Christopher, M., McDonald, M. and Wills, C., 'Introducing Marketing' (Pan).
[6] Zimmerman, G. W., 'The ABCs of Vilfredo Pareto', *Production and Inventory Management*, September 1975.

The accountant and marketing management

The strategic nature of marketing management's budget responsibilities in the overall budgeting process highlights the fact that marketing today is much more sophisticated than the limited area which was traditionally envisaged as marketing. There is a great need for the generation of quantitative information related to marketing. It is, therefore, of prime importance that Marketing and Financial Managers co-ordinate, co-operate and communicate effectively. Thus, the financial implications of various marketing strategies must be very carefully considered, and this will necessitate co-ordination with other functions, production distribution, research and development, etc.

Co-ordination between marketing and finance is, however, hindered by people problems. A 'cultural lag' has been identified between the finance function and other disciplines. There appears to be resistance (from accountants) to change, and a failure to take a more sophisticated view, especially in the areas of costing and valuation. The reasons put forward for the occurrence of such a cultural lag are as follows:

1 The views held by members of each of the professions concerned about the other: the marketing manager may well describe the accountant as 'rather formal and difficult to approach. His undoubted professionalism sometimes seems designed to stifle rather than encourage enterprise. He is not to be trusted too far, and his social conscience leaves something to be desired.'

   The accountant on the other hand may view the marketing manager as follows: 'He is a bit of a rogue, not very bright, rather less reliable than others, and his accuracy is definitely suspect. He is a shade more professional than his personnel manager friend, but slumps to the bottom again where social responsibility is concerned.'

   These attitudes add to the behavioural problems encountered during the co-ordination process.

2 That it occurs when one element of culture changes more rapidly than another. In business and professional fields this occurs when knowledge developed in one field takes several years to filter down and affect practice. Alternatively, knowledge which is available in a particular field may not be applied to or integrated with functionally related theory and practice in a neighbouring discipline where some elements are interdependent, and where there has been rapid change. The latter has occurred in the case of accounting in trying to meet the needs of the new marketing concept.

Many accountants believe that they have fulfilled their management responsibilities when, by acting as devil's advocates, they succeeded in keeping the marketing director down-to-earth. One would not mind so much if, in doing so, the accountant had access to meaningful facts and figures which had been carefully researched. But in the majority of instances this is not the case. Thus, in recent times examples can be found of apparently sound companies in financial difficulties because there was a lack of financial expertise in the formulation of marketing policies. Without financial discipline in the assessment and evaluation of marketing policies, companies operate at their own peril. If the accountants do not learn to speak with authority in marketing, other professions will take back the initiative and leadership which the accountancy profession gained in the 1960s.

The findings of a survey done by the American Accounting Association (1972) indicated that it is not unusual for a firm's accounting system to be of little direct help to the decision-making and control process of marketing management. However, this does not mean that the accounting function is incapable of supplying relevant data. Rather, it indicates that most accounting systems are not currently designed to meet the specific needs of marketing management.

Accounting systems were developed to report the aggregate effect of a firm's operations to its shareholders and other interested parties. In more recent times, accounting systems have been redesigned to meet the needs of management. The net result, however, is an accounting system oriented towards external reporting and production cost analysis. There has been a tendency on the part of accountants to ignore cost and management accounting problems, relating to the marketing area or to apply similar methods to those used in the production area. The accountant cannot merely transfer the tools developed in production to marketing as a total system. He must start with the fundamentals, and he or she may have to abandon many of the stereotyped approaches used by accountants in planning and control.

Since the introduction of the new marketing concept and its rapidly growing implementation, marketing managers have had to make decisions of increasing variety and complexity guided by criteria such as:

a) Increase in sales volume or market share.
b) Maintenance of a 'complete' product line.
c) Rapid penetration of a market, and
d) Suitability of a product to the organisation's capabilities.

In trying to meet the needs of such 'marketing' criteria, marketers are beginning to require constructive use of 'financial' criteria such as cost-volume-profit analysis and return on investment. This gives recognition to the basic objective of numerous business firms, i.e. to maximise shareholders' return on their investment imposed by competition, government, unions, and public opinion. Therefore, finance and marketing should be inseparably linked in the business system. On the other hand, it may be argued that marketing is the *part* of management thinking concerned with making decisions about a market place.

Management accounting is also fundamental to management decisions in providing some of the necessary information. Both fields are defined and therefore justified by their contribution to the management task. Therefore, the management objective at any particular time determines the contribution which is needed from each.

Given this argument, it would appear that a *general* business training is needed and the professions of accounting and marketing cannot, in the interests of organisations, be kept apart. There is a great need for accountants to join with other professions to effect improvements to the decision making process.

Why was the financial/marketing interface not developed? Some of the answers may be provided by a quite recent study carried out in Australia. This identified the following restrictive factors:

a) Accountants lack the knowledge and understanding of the information requirements necessary for the marketing function.
b) Accountants do not accept marketing as a distinct and separate managerial function. This reinforces the 'cultural lag' problem discussed earlier.

c) Organisational design may impede adequate communications between functions. This could (and does) happen to such an extent that the accounting and marketing departments may be geographically diverse from one another.

Restriction a) above is an indication of the need to bridge the knowledge gap by providing relevant marketing education. For qualified accountants this need could well be catered for by continuing professional education short courses, articles in the accounting journals, and suitable post-graduate courses. With regard to the future generation of accountants the attack is really threefold.

1 Undergraduate courses in business schools.
2 Increasing the marketing content of the professional examinations. This process commenced several years ago.
3 Short courses, including a marketing input to induction courses.

Over time, and with satisfactory educational progress, the second restriction should eventually be overcome. For the time being, however, barriers between the two functions will continue to exist. Marketing management also need financial and management accounting knowledge, in order to understand the accountant's point of view. In many cases this need is already met, because the Institute of Marketing include an accounting paper in their diploma examinations.

The third restriction covers an area which is being studied by behavioural scientists. However, this area does feature in the Institute of Marketing's examinations and in certain papers of professional accountancy examinations. This is also an area in which accountants and others have a knowledge gap, but that is another story. Suffice it to say that tomorrow's accountant cannot ignore behavioural science.

In recent years there has from time to time appeared in the professional press, advertisements asking for marketing accountants; management accountants with marketing knowledge; marketing managers with a finance background; etc. Therefore, very slowly, the need for financial controls in marketing is being realised by the larger companies, and thus they require suitably qualified personnel.

The *marketing accountant* is not only involved in cost analysis, cost control, budgeting and variance analysis; but is also involved in providing information and controlling all aspects of the marketing mix such as product management, pricing, marketing research, promotional strategy, salesmen's motivation, sales management, distribution, product abandonment, and credit management. Thus, he plays more the role of 'controller' than of 'accountant'. The principal responsibility of such an accountant is to evaluate alternative uses of company funds and to act as a balance wheel in the competition between sections/departments for those funds.

Marketing management proposals are likely to be optimistic. The accountant has, therefore, to critically review each request for funds and compare it with the alternative uses of funds in other parts of the company. Areas of conflict are minimised to the extent to which requests are supported by facts and figures.

The other responsibilities of the marketing accountant may include the following:

a) Maintaining the required liquidity levels for the numerous segments of the company.
b) Keeping the firm in healthy fiscal shape so that it may compete for funds with confidence.
c) Understanding the short-term and long-term financial implications of different marketing segments.
d) Appraisal of marketing performance.
e) Making sure that financial information relating to marketing ties up with the 'management information system' of the company.

In conclusion, both financial and marketing management need to be better acquainted with the concepts and techniques of financially controlling marketing activities. Continuing professional education, educational establishments and professional journals have a vital role to play in bridging the knowledge gap, and overcoming the cultural gap. Barriers must be broken down, co-ordination and communication improved and all business functions must learn to work together in harmony.

5

Capital investment appraisal

Many of the books which attempt to cover this subject do not devote a lot of time and effort to the question of selecting the discount rate. As this can have a significant effect upon the outcome, there is a need to attempt to provide an answer to the question of which discount rate should be used? The first reading in this chapter attempts to do just that.

I have encountered quite a number of methods devised for taking into account the tax factor. Many of these methods, possibly as a result of trying to over-simplify, I am sorry to say tend to confuse, especially when dealing with real-world-type examples. See what you think of the method which I have devised.

A lot of student type practice problems tend to promote ideas such as:

If the net present value is positive then accept the project.

What tends to happen is that certain non-financial factors are ignored and this is the theme of the third reading 'Money doesn't mean everything'. I would like to see projects being described as being worthy of consideration if at the end of the financial computations, they end up with a positive NPV. After all, the financial data is just one component part of the capital invest-ment decision-making process. This should be clear to you when you have read the articles which have been reproduced in this chapter and after a study of the diagram included in 'The planning and evaluating of capital in-vestments'.

Capital investment appraisal – which discount rate?

'I propose that we evaluate this particular project using the discounted cash flow approach,' said the Production Director.

'And which discount rate would you propose that we use?' commented the Finance Director.

'Oh, I think that we can quite easily leave all of that in the capable hands of your accounts department', interrupted the Managing Director.

How true a reflection is this, of your own situation and experience?

It is an indisputable fact that in the real world of industry and commerce accountants are frequently confronted with the problem of selecting an appropriate discount rate. It is, however, unlikely that a lot of time and thought is devoted to this highly subjective area. The selection of a discount rate is a time consuming and complex process.

Why discount?

Money has a 'time value', i.e. a £1 today will be worth more than a £1 in the future: using a 10 per cent discount rate £1 today will be worth 90.9p in one year's time.

This is caused by a number of factors such as consumer preferences, investment opportunities, risk and impact of inflation.[1]

The discounting technique provides the accountant with a method by which cash flows can be adjusted to take into account the time value of money.

Discounting the cash flow, it must be said, is just one of a number of factors which must be assessed during the capital investment decision-making process, e.g. there are numerous non-financial factors.[2]

The selection of a discount rate

There are a multitude of rates from which a selection can be made.

The cost of capital

'Oh, as a rule of thumb, I would just use the cost of capital as our discount rate', propounded the Company Secretary.

This simplistic approach is just not on. Quite a number of authorities advocate the adoption of the cost of capital as an appropriate discount rate. The principal concern here arises from the fact that there are in existence several ways of computing a company's cost of capital. One further complication is that a decision will have to be reached about whether to use the before- or after-tax cost of capital!

The weighted average cost of capital is a method which reflects the current gearing and tends to be used in cases where the same structural financial mix is going to continue.

If the gearing is likely to change in the future, then it would seem that the anticipated future weighted average cost of capital would be preferable.

It is difficult to determine changes to the future structural mix, e.g. caused by environmental change such as competition, economic, political and technological factors. The weighting may be based on book values or market values (see Fig. 5.1, p. 143). However, it is generally agreed that a cost based on market values may give a more accurate picture in times of changing values.

Figure 5.1 illustrates that differences between the two methods can occur. Such differences could be quite significant! The computation of the cost figures via the formulae is open to differing interpretations and highly debatable. Growth rates have to be pre-determined, taxation must be taken into account and market price/market value selections made. In addition to affecting a company's gearing, any new financing may also have an impact upon the company's risk profile.

An alternative to the weighted average cost method is to use the marginal cost method.

The marginal cost of capital is the total change in the cost of the finance incurred through a new project. This method is considered to be appropriate in cases where a project is financed from a specific source and the source utilised does not correspond to the financing proportions that the firm intends to use in the future.

It is, however, extremely difficult to identify the cost of financing a particular project, because several projects may be commissioned at the same time, using finance from a variety of sources.

The cost of capital, weighted or marginal, as a discount rate is useful in that if the project under review achieves a positive net present value (NPV) it is worthy of further consideration. The cost of capital is, as indicated, a highly subjective area.

Cut-off rates

A frequently adopted alternative to the cost of capital as the discount rate is the cut-off rate. Management have to agree upon the cut-off rate/s to be employed. This method is useful in times of capital rationing and where numerous projects have to be screened. Projects with a negative NPV are automatically rejected and those with positive NPVs proceed for further consideration. A drawback to this method is that projects which fall below the cut-off but above their cost of capital are simply ignored.

Risk-adjusted discount rates

There are a number of ways in which the risk factor may be dealt with. The cut-off method can be extended to take the project's risk category into account. It is therefore, possible that companies employ differential cut-offs, e.g.

Project risk	Discount rate
Low	12%
Average	17%
High	25%

Thus, the higher the risk, the higher the discount rate. Risk assessment is a difficult matter and here also, subjectivity is brought into play. This method is suitable for real world situations. Management do, in fact, have to make their selections from numerous projects with differing classifications.

Internal rate of return

'Why not dispense with the discount rate/NPV approach and simply evaluate alternatives according to their respective internal rates of return?' said the Management Accountant.

A very good question. This would free the personnel concerned from having to decide upon which discount rate to adopt. Projects can be ranked according to their internal rate of return (IRR) and risk category. A quite recent survey indicated that this technique has found wide acceptance in the real world.[3] Of the firms surveyed 41 per cent were using IRR as their primary method of appraisal.

Cash flows

It should be noted that cash flows which are being discounted are only estimates. Their calculation should, one hopes, have taken inflation and taxation into account. Cash flows, it must also be pointed out, do not accrue evenly throughout the year and it may be necessary to adjust discount rates accordingly.

It would appear that a perception of accuracy occurs when the cash flows are multiplied by the discount factor. Beware, the cash flows are still estimates and the discount factor the outcome of subjective judgement.

Guidelines and conclusions

The selection of an appropriate discount rate should therefore, take into account the following considerations:

a) The weighted average method is suitable for situations where the current financing structural mix is going to continue. Where that mix is likely to change, an attempt should be made at calculating the anticipated cost of the new structure.

b) Weighted averages based on market values tend to give a better reflection of the cost of capital during periods of changing values, i.e. the usual real world situation.

c) If at all possible, identify the source/cost of the funds which will be used to finance a particular project.

d) Do not ignore the risk factor. Take risk into account, e.g. by adjusting discount rates accordingly.

e) We live in a world with taxation, so take the impact of tax into account when computing the discount rate.

f) The discounting process is just one component part of the capital investment decision making process. It is most certainly not the 'be all and end all'.

g) It does not matter which discount rate is used, if the cash flows are way out of line and based upon improper assumptions.

h) The adoption of the internal rate of return technique avoids many of the problems associated with the selection of discount rates. It is a method which merits attention.

i) A post-audit/monitoring process should be instigated to provide management with valuable feedback upon projects in progress.

On the face of it, it would appear that the selection of an appropriate discount rate is an easy matter. This is not so, subjective judgements are never easy and several variables have to be considered. The only certainty is that it will continue to puzzle and perplex the accountancy profession for many years to come.

Which discount rate do you use?

Book values

Weighted average cost of capital

(a)	(b)	(c)	(d)	(e)
Method	Book value £m	Proportion %	Cost £	Weighted cost, £ (c×d)
Debentures	30	30	(a) 5	1.5
Preference	20	20	(b) 8	1.6
Ordinary	30	30	(c)12	3.6
Retained	20	20	(d)10	2.0
Earnings	100	100		8.7

Market values

(a)	(b)	(c)	(d)	(e)
Method	Market value £m	Proportion %	Cost £	Weighted cost, £ (c×d)
Debentures	30	20.00	(a) 5	1.00
Preference	20	13.33	(b) 8	1.07
Equity	100	66.67	(c)12	8.00
	150	100		10.07

Fig. 5.1 Weighted costs of capital calculated using book values and market values

The above cost figures have been arrived at by employing the following formulae:

a) Debentures $= \dfrac{\text{coupon rate}}{\text{current market price}} \times (1 - \text{tax rate})$

b) Preference shares $= \dfrac{\text{coupon rate}}{\text{market price}} \times 100$

c) New equity (ordinary) $= \dfrac{\text{dividend per share}}{(\text{market price} - \text{issue costs})} + \text{growth rate}$

d) Retained earnings $= \dfrac{\text{dividend per share}}{\text{market price}} + \text{growth rate}$

143

References
[1]Pike, R. H. and Dobbins, R. *Investment Decisions and Financial Strategy* (Philip Allan Publishers, 1986).
[2]Chadwick, L. 'Money doesn't mean everything'. *Accountants Weekly* 12 June 1981.
[3]Pike, R. H. *Capital Budgeting in the 1980s* (ICMA, 1982).

Further reading
Knott, G., *Understanding Financial Management* (Pan, 1985).

Capital investment appraisal and the tax factor

The tax factor always has, and always will, play an important role in the capital investment decision making process. In view of the fact that first year capital allowances on plant and machinery have now been phased out (Table 28), one would think that taxation would have little impact. This is not the case. Many commentators, managers and students tend to talk as though all of the capital allowances relating to plant and machinery have been axed. However, it must be remembered that the 25 per cent writing down allowance is still available. It is allowable from the first year in which the expenditure takes place on cost and from the second year onwards on the written down value brought forward. This reducing balance method of capital allowances is no stranger, it has been in use for years and years in the area of cars capable of private use. In the year of sale, no writing down allowances are computed and claimed. The sale proceeds received are compared with the plant and machinery's written down value brought forward. The difference between the two figures being a balancing charge (on a profit on sale) or a balancing allowance (resulting from a loss on sale), tax being payable on any balancing charge or repayable on any balancing allowance.

I have observed quite a number of off-beat attempts at computing the taxation impact upon the discounted cash flow method of capital investment appraisal. To my mind, taxation should be taken into account during the process of estimating the incremental cash flows. After all, cash flow is all about time lags, i.e. the points in time when cash comes in or goes out. Taxation, from a cash point of view is no different. There is a time lag between the tax being paid/repaid and the income being generated.

Table 28: Rates of first year capital allowances on plant and machinery

	Rate
Up to 13 March 1984	100%
14 March 1984 to 31 March 1985	75%
1 April 1985 to 31 March 1986	50%
On and after 1 April 1986	Nil

I would like to propose that the following systematic method be considered, not just from an exam technique point of view but also from a practical point of view:

a) Estimate the incremental cash flows (excluding taxation effects).
b) Work out the capital allowances over the life of the project taking into account the estimated residual value of the plant and machinery at the end of the project.
c) Deduct the capital allowances from the incremental cash flow, and then work out the tax payable or repayable by multiplying the net taxable incremental cash flow by the appropriate rate of Corporation Tax. You have now calculated the tax payable/repayable.
d) Taking into account the time lag for the payment/repayment of tax deduct the tax payable or add the tax repayable to the appropriate incremental cash flows (taxable and non taxable).
e) Select an appropriate discount rate taking into account the tax factor. This is not an easy task and requires a great deal of time and thought.

Mini case study

The following mini case study using real world tax rates should help with the quest towards gaining an understanding of the impact of taxation upon the capital investment decision.

Your company, Ingwik PLC, is considering disposing of an old machine and replacing it by purchasing a new and more efficient machine.

You are provided with the following information:

The old machine

Life	6 years
Purchased	4 years ago
Cost	£36 000
Residual value 1 July 1987	£3000
Tax written down value	Nil
Book value (after depreciating at $\frac{1}{6}$ per annum straight line)	£12 000
Residual value at the end of its life, i.e. end of year 31 December 1988	Nil

The new machine

Life	(approx)	5 years
Cost		£84 000
Residual value at the end of 31.9.1991		£14 000

Depreciation at $\frac{1}{5}$ per annum straight line will be charged.

Date of purchase The company is proposing to buy the machine on 1 July 1987.

Taxation assumptions

a) If the machine is purchased outright capital allowances will be available at the appropriate rates.
b) Tax payments (and refunds, if any) are made in the year following that to which they relate.

c) The company's rates of corporation tax are those which are applicable to large companies.

Cost of capital The company's net of tax cost of capital is 10 per cent.

Incremental cost savings are estimated to be as follows:

Year	New machine purchased
31.12.1987	£12 000
31.12.1988	£23 000
31.12.1989	£39 000
31.12.1990	£37 000
31.12.1991	£21 000

You are required to prepare discounted cash flow statements and advise your company as to which course of action should be taken.

Suggested solution

Step 1 The estimated incremental cash flows excluding the effect of taxation have already been computed.

Step 2 The computation of the capital allowances.*

Year ending	Cost of written down value b/f	Writing down allowance @25%	Written down value (WDV) c/f
	£	£	£
31.12.87	84 000	21 000	63 000
31.12.88	63 000	15 750	47 250
31.12.89	47 250	11 813	35 437
31.12.90	35 437	8 859	26 578

Year ending 31.12.87 Disposal of old machine

Sale proceeds	£3000
less	
Tax written down value	Nil
Balancing charge	£3000

Year ending 31.12.91 Disposal of new machine

Sale proceeds	£14 000
less	
Tax written down value	26 578
Balancing allowance	£12 578

*Note that depreciation, being a non-cash item, does not have any effect whatsoever upon the outcome

146

Step 3 *Calculation of the tax payable/repayable*

	a)	b)	c)	d)	e)
Year ending	Cash flow	Capital allowances	Net taxable cash flow (a − b)	Rate of corporation tax	Tax (payable)/ repayable (c × d)
	£	£	£		£
31.12.87	12 000	18 000*	(6 000)	35%	2100 Refund
31.12.88	23 000	15 750	7 250	35%	(2537)
31.12.89	39 000	11 813	27 187	35%	(9515)
31.12.90	37 000	8 859	28 141	35%	(9849)
31.12.91	21 000	12 578 (BA)	8 422	35%	(2948)

*(£21 000 less £3000 balancing charge)

Step 4 *The discounted cash flow computation*

Year ending	Cash flow	Tax (payable)/ repayable	Net	Net of tax discount rate	DCF
	£	(Approx 1 year)	£		£
31.12.87	12 000	(Time Lag)	12 000	0.909	10 908
31.12.88	23 000	2100	25 100	0.826	20 733
31.12.89	39 000	(2537)	36 463	0.751	27 384
31.12.90	37 000	(9515)	27 485	0.683	18 772
31.12.91	35 000*	(9849)	25 151	0.621	15 619
31.12.92	-	(2948)	(2 948)	0.564	(1 663)
					91 753

less Initial cost (£84 000 less amount received for old machine £3000)   81 000

Net present value   10 753

*21 000 + residual value of new machine £14 000

Note

a) The discount rates for 31.12.87 and 31.12.91 could be amended to take into account the fact that the periods covered by the cash flows are six months and nine months, respectively.
b) It is a very difficult task to estimate the incremental cash flows.
c) It is possibly even more difficult to estimate the future residual value of plant and machinery. Because of unforeseen advances in technology the machine considered in this mini-case could be significantly less than the figure currently estimated.
d) The actual date on which the tax would be paid over could vary considerably because of audit delays/appeals, etc.
e) There are many factors other than the financial factors which must be taken into account during the capital investment decision-making process.

147

Conclusion

In the capital investment decision the tax factor must not and should not be ignored.

Money doesn't mean everything: The non-financial aspects of capital investment appraisal

'The return on the project is greater than the firm's cost of capital, I therefore recommend acceptance of the project.' Is the capital investment decision really so easy and clear cut? There is a real danger of accountants being so preoccupied with the financial aspects of capital investment appraisal that they may ignore other very important factors. Although these factors omitted may be described as non-financial and subject to qualitative decisions they could have quite a marked effect upon the firm's long term financial performance.

The various methods used by accountants to evaluate projects do have a number of limitations. Cash flows have to be estimated and will most certainly not accrue evenly throughout the years in question. The choice of discount rate (e.g. used in the Net Present Value Method) is subjective, although certain authorities do recommend that the firm's cost of capital should be used. However, one could ask the question 'which cost of capital?'. There are a number of different cost of capital figures which could be used (e.g. current cost; weighted average cost; estimated future cost) and these are subject to different interpretations relating to their calculation. The assessment of risk presents additional problems (e.g. which probability factor to use) and is dependent upon the subjective judgement of the individual.

'The estimated cash flows multiplied by the discount factor make the resultant figures more accurate.' The message to be derived from this apparently absurd statement is that management may become so involved with the method of assessment that they tend to ignore the limitations referred to above. This means that they may in fact be regarding the figures as more accurate than they really are. The information generated from any such assessment can only be as accurate as the original input. Management must therefore appreciate that the financial information is just one small component part of the capital investment decision. Unfortunately accountants cannot foretell the future, e.g. estimated future cash flows will be affected by a multitude of unforeseen factors. The only certainty about the future is the fact that it will be uncertain.

Cash flows can be significantly affected by any trade-in received for the old equipment and the method adopted for financing the project, e.g. HP; leasing, etc. This means that for each alternative being considered there could be a number of different cash flow patterns.

The non-financial factors

In addition to the financial aspects of the capital investment decision there are also many other areas which warrant attention such as:

1 Technical

a) The need for technical superiority.
b) Flexibility and adaptability.
c) Ease of maintenance.
d) Operational considerations, e.g. need to retrain/recruit personnel.
e) Servicing arrangements.
f) Manuals provided for operating and servicing.
g) Peripherals necessary for efficient operation or adding at some future date. It is not unheard of for an organisation to purchase equipment and find that they are unable to use it without first buying certain peripherals.
h) Capacity.

2 Imported equipment

Exchange rates may affect the position dramatically depending upon the method of payment adopted. An important question which must be answered is 'How good is the supplier's servicing and availability of spares in the UK?' It may be first class in the supplier's own country but very poor in the UK. Other considerations under this heading involve:

a) The additional administration necessary to deal with the additional documentation and foreign exchange.
b) Delays in delivery of the equipment and spares caused by air and sea transportation problems and political instability.

3 Size and weight of equipment

Floors may need strengthening and walls may have to be knocked down and rebuilt to accommodate the equipment. This possibility will affect the cash flows and should not be overlooked.

4 Standardisation of equipment

The benefits of obtaining similar equipment from a tried and tested supplier can have profound consequences upon the financial analysis. Savings should be possible in the areas of operative training, ease of maintenance and inventory of spares, e.g. one component may fit several different machines.

5 Look before you buy

It may well be worth the time and expense to actually inspect the equipment in a working environment. The opportunity to talk with operatives and personnel involved with such equipment should certainly not be neglected.

6 Human and social factors

Firms who ignore such factors as safety, noise, fumes, etc. in today's complex and diverse business environment do so at their peril. The financial consequences of ignoring them could be catastrophic.

149

7 Organisational behaviour

The effects of 'people problems' upon an organisation cannot and should not be underestimated. This area alone could jeopardise the success of the whole venture for reasons such as:

a) Resistance to change, e.g. introducing new technology.
b) Empire building, e.g. where sub-unit goals conflict with the organisation's own goals.
c) Perceptions about what the management want.
d) Organisational structure, e.g. certain personnel may be in control of key information junctions or have direct access to top management.
e) The boardroom balance of power, e.g. finance versus engineers.

There are, of course, numerous other factors that need to be taken into account, e.g. special offers – two for the price of one; guarantees; and the possibility of renegotiating the terms.

Thus, the so called non-financial factors may have a significant influence upon a firm's long term financial performance and cannot be ignored in the capital investment decision-making process.

The planning and evaluating of capital investments

The essential elements of a system for planning and evaluating capital investments are as follows:

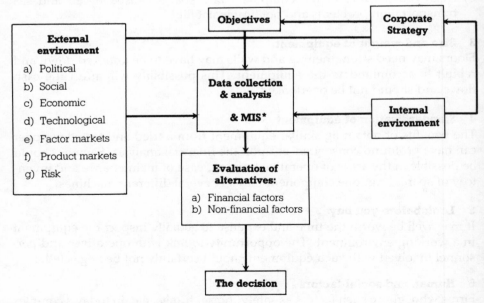

*MIS=Management Information System.

Fig. 5.2 *The capital investment decision*

a) *Objectives*

All projects should be in line with the objectives/policy of the company concerned. In particular, the company's objectives relating to the required return on capital employed should be clearly stated and understood.

b) *Data collection and analysis*

Data has to be collected, classified, analysed and presented in a form appropriate to the needs and understanding of the user. A key decision that has to be made is the method(s) by which the investment is to be appraised, e.g. Discounted Cash Flow.

c) *The Management Information System*

The provision of relevant and appropriate information to management can most certainly enhance the decision-making process. An effective Management Information System is therefore a prerequisite to aid efficient planning and control. The quality of the information will help to determine the accuracy of forecasts relating to future performance. However, it is possible to provide management with too much information, 'information overload', which tends to weigh them down. The quality of the information rather than quantity is therefore closely linked to the quality of the decision making.

d) *Monitoring the external environment*

The external environment in which a firm operates is so diverse and complex that it must be subjected to continuous monitoring. This will reveal threats and opportunities which could, at a stroke, change the whole nature of a firm's capital investment programme, e.g. political instability in the country of a major customer.

e) *Evaluation*

In addition to the financial factors which have to be examined management must also take various non-financial factors into account, e.g. availability of spare parts, flexibility, standardisation, etc.

f) *The internal environment*

The firm cannot ignore its own internal environment, an analysis of which will indicate strengths and weaknesses, e.g. industrial relations, idle capacity. The acceptance by workers of new plant and new processes can be of principal importance and should not be overlooked.

Once a decision to go ahead with an investment has been taken, that is not the end of the story. The investment should be carefully monitored, and changes to the environment, internal and external, in which the firm operates cannot be ignored. Companies must be able to change more rapidly to meet enforced changed circumstances if they are to survive and prosper.

6

Other issues

The readings in this final chapter should be of general interest to most readers.

Two of the readings take a look at the financial aspects of centralised and decentralised distribution. The third reading takes a brief look at the subject of pricing. It was considered that to go into greater depth in this area was outside the scope of this publication; the objective being to include some introductory material on the subject.

Vfm (value for money auditing) has really taken off in the UK public sector. The article which is reproduced in this section attempts to promote the use of vfm in the private sector.

The final reading in this book about ZBB (zero-base budgeting) is designed to make you aware of its existence and to explain what it is and how it works.

The financial aspects of centralised distribution

Over the past ten years the role of distribution management has increased in importance. Effective distribution management is needed to counteract ever increasing costs and legislative burdens, e.g. driver hours, health and safety, etc. Frequent changes in the diverse and complex business environment in which the firm operates necessitates the need for the competent management of the distribution function. As with other areas of business management, there are very rarely any easy decisions, just 'trade-offs'.

What works for one company may not work for another. Methods and systems cannot always be easily transferable from company to company, industry to industry and country to country. In the final analysis, management must decide. They must base their decisions on the best available relevant data and take account of both financial and non-financial factors, i.e. quantitative and qualitative factors.

Centralised distribution

When deciding the direction in which a company should develop its distribution operations there are two main options available for consideration. One is based around a centralised policy and the other is a more regionalised solution.

A centralised distribution system occurs when the company concerned makes all of its deliveries from one main depot. This would consist of the handling and storage facilities, the base for the company's vehicles and the administration centre (see Fig. 6.1).

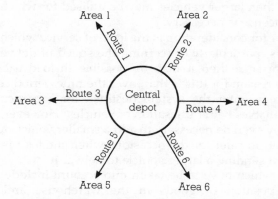

Fig. 6.1 *This demonstrates centralised distribution where all vehicles are based at one depot and deliver to different areas of the country from there*

If the company adopts a regional policy this would entail establishing, or obtaining, depots in each of the regions to which they deliver in sufficient quantities. There would still probably be one main depot (usually the original one or the largest one) at which overall control is maintained and at which the majority of the administration is carried out.

Unfortunately the decision between a centralised or regional operation is much more complicated than is indicated by first impressions, and is not simply a case of whether the company has a sufficient volume of goods to deliver to justify opening a depot in a particular area of the country.

Which factors must be taken into account?

If the decision is made to concentrate on a centralised distribution policy then several variables have to be considered before the system is brought into operation.

First, it is necessary to recognise which area of the market the company operates in and, consequently, for what type of goods the distribution system is supposed to cater. The outcome of this decision affects other variables such as the storage and handling facilities that it will be necessary to employ and the type of vehicles required. If the goods are to be reasonably light and cartonised then a conveyor system around the storage warehouse could prove to be a worthwhile investment. If they are heavy items then a forklift, or other similar lifting apparatus, may be necessary, along with some open floor space for their storage to which a forklift has access.

If the majority of the work is through light, cartonised traffic then the 7.5 tonne gross weight vehicles, which can be driven by anyone possessing a normal car driver's licence, will probably satisfy the requirements of the company.

The body size of the vehicle can be determined depending on whether the cartons are light and bulky. If the goods carried are heavy, or extremely bulky, or the deliveries required exceed the capacity of a 7.5 tonne gross weight vehicle, then larger vehicles may be utilised for which a heavy goods vehicle (HGV) licence is necessary.

Another factor for consideration is the level of service which is to be offered to the customers, particularly concerning the speed of delivery. If time is of secondary importance then it may be possible to load each vehicle more effectively. One reason for this is that, over the time period concerned, more consignments may enter the system destined for a particular area of the country which enables better utilisation of vehicles. However, if a fast service is required it may even be necessary to add a smaller vehicle to the fleet, such as a Ford Transit, to cater for the occasions when the load is so small that it does not warrant sending a larger vehicle to deliver it.

Other factors which have to be taken into account include the methods of recording the position of goods in the warehouse and other general administrational processes. The design and processing of system input documents, vehicle load lists and consignment notes, and invoices must also be considered. The decisions in this area will help to determine the type of staff which need to be employed and the company's internal systems regarding communications, for example, to release goods for delivery.

Why opt for centralised distribution?

Centralised distribution has its advantages but is by no means infallible, and is not always the optimal type of system for a company to employ.

Control

One of the most advantageous aspects of centralised distribution is that it allows complete control of the system to be maintained through a single depot. This includes the control of all goods which are carried because they are only ever in the one warehouse and usually stay in the same place from arrival to final departure for delivery. The security side of the operation should be easier to implement and organise. It should also be more effective in that it is certainly more practical to control than a regional system.

Vehicles

It should result in better control of vehicles operated in terms of maintenance and utilisation. The stocks of spare parts should be lower than for a regional system. This would bring about savings in capital tied up in stocks, interest charges and associated holding costs.

Communication

A further advantage is that any communication within the company is done at closer range because of the proximity of the different departments. This creates fewer opportunities for mistakes to be made as a result of misunderstandings, or other breakdowns in the system, which occasionally occur if there is a high level of communication between different depots or departments in different areas of the country.

Personnel

Most of the people employed by the company will originate from the same area. If people know their fellow workers well this tends to aid internal communication and once again, reduce the incidence of mistakes. Also, concerning employees, centralised distribution allows for a consistent policy of appointments because the same people usually conduct the interviews when vacancies occur within the organisation. A company which uses this method of distribution is more likely to be in a position to employ more specialists and highly qualified staff. Thus, there should be savings in personnel costs and increased efficiency, which it is hoped would be brought about by the employment of specialists.

What are the drawbacks?

One of the major faults with centralised distribution is due to the very nature of its operation in that it is based at one depot in one area of the country. This means that any vehicles delivering goods to another part of the country have to start their journey from the depot and either finish there or stay away from home for the night (due to the limitations placed on drivers' hours). If a driver and his vehicle do have to stay out overnight this results in quite considerable increases in the costs which have to be absorbed by the goods he is carrying. Not only are there the vehicle and driver costs for two days but also the extra overnight expenses which most companies pay their drivers to cover accommodation and the parking of the vehicle.

Another problem is the necessity to employ warehousing facilities large enough to enable the storage at the central depot of all the goods processed by the company. This leads to high fixed costs, overhead and administrational costs due to the size of the building required. There is also the possibility that goods could be mislaid more easily in a large warehouse.

As a result of the company being based in one part of the country this effectively restricts it to concentrating on obtaining work from that area. It is more difficult for it to take on contracts based in areas away from its central depot because the goods will invariably have to be returned there before they can be redistributed. This tends to be time-consuming and costly because the consignments may eventually be carried many more miles than would be necessary if the work were done by a more local haulier. The result is that the company either charges rates which are too expensive because of the work involved or receives little or no contribution from these deliveries.

A further fault is that it does not always allow for a reliably quick service.

For example, problems could arise if a company only delivers to a particular part of the country once weekly because of the small number of consignments for that area. If goods arrive at the depot the same day as the vehicle has been despatched on the route concerned they have to wait for at least a week before the next delivery. For many customers this time lapse would prove to be unacceptable and work may be lost because of it.

Unless a distribution company advertises the fact that it specialises in deliveries to only one area of the country, it will invariably receive consignments destined for places to which it does not normally deliver. This often results in a loss being made to ensure that the goods are delivered within an acceptable period of time. In other words, profit is forgone in order to maintain service. This problem is experienced by most companies who operate centralised distribution and is a further fault with the system.

The use of sub-contractors

The use of one or more sub-contractors may offer the company an alternative to the operation of the less profitable routes which are included in their service.

If the company has only a small number of deliveries to a certain area of the country it may prove costly to maintain the service levels required by those customers, often to the extent of making a considerable loss. If such deliveries were evaluated in isolation the routes concerned would often be discontinued. However, these consignments often originate from contracts which consist mainly of goods to be delivered via the more profitable routes and such contracts are usually only retained because of the service offered by the company which covers all areas of the country. Consequently, if the less profitable (or loss-making) route was to be discontinued it may result in the loss of several lucrative contracts and a severe reduction in workload.

An alternative solution which enables the company to maximise the use of its own resources by concentrating on those areas in which it operates most effectively, whilst reducing the losses incurred on its less efficient routes, is the use of sub-contractors. This entails using the services of another distribution company which specialises in delivering to the area concerned. For example, if Company A is based in Luton and specialises in deliveries to the South of England there are three alternative services which it could utilise to have goods delivered to Manchester. First, there is Company B, which is also situated in Luton but which specialises in deliveries to the North of England. Secondly there is Company C which operates a nationwide regionally based distribution service and has depots both in Luton and in several places in the North of England. Thirdly there is Company D which is actually based in the North of England and delivers mainly in that area but also has a regular service to the South of England which always passes through, or close to, Luton.

Any one of these three options could be exploited by Company A to improve its profitability. In fact it could not only be used to improve the service offered but also to provide one in the first place if one does not exist.

Therefore it is possible for a company to specialise in only one area but to have one nationwide company or a network of sub-contractors to cover the rest of the country.

If a sufficient quantity of goods is channelled through any one sub-contractor it may be possible to negotiate reduced rates which enable the company to actually make a profit on the deliveries rather than making a loss or just covering costs to maintain the service.

The biggest disadvantage with using sub-contractors is that, if they discover the initial source of the goods they are delivering, they may try to approach the customer themselves in order to cut out the profit of the company who originally gave them the deliveries. This may result in the loss of the whole contract if the sub-contractor offers a reduced price or a better service to the customer than the original company could.

Conclusions

Central distribution has many advantages but it also has quite a number of faults. Every case is unique and must be based on its merits. Whatever the system employed, it must be subjected to frequent reviews in order to keep pace with the changes which have taken or are about to take place in the environment. Such changes may be economic, social, technological, political or relate to factor and/or product markets. It is therefore important that all these areas are monitored to ensure that management can take speedy but appropriate action.

The financial aspects of decentralised distribution

The theoretical extreme in the case of decentralised distribution would involve the company concerned in having a depot in each geographic area to which it delivered. Each depot would then attempt to attract business regardless of final destination. However, of the various combinations systems operating in the real world, two can be identified.

The first of these employs a central main depot, e.g. in the Midlands, plus a number of other depots in the regions served by the company (see Fig. 6.2). The idea of this particular system is that all goods which are destined for some other region will pass to that region via the central depot. Goods for the area covered by the particular regional depot will be separated and processed ready for their distribution. The remaining goods will be sent to the central depot/head office. The central depot will then sort, allocate and deliver the goods to the appropriate regional depots. The regional depots will then deliver the goods to their final destination. This should ensure that goods going from the central depot to the regions are transported in economic consignments. It should also provide management with an easier-to-operate system for controlling inter-regional transactions.

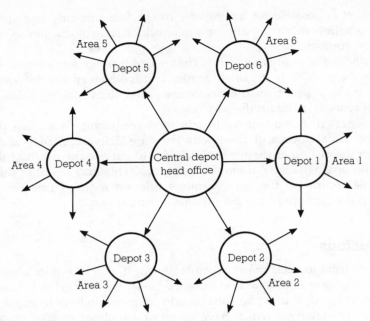

Fig. 6.2 *Regional distribution with a central depot through which all goods destined for other regions pass.*

The second alternative occurs when the system deals with sufficient goods to justify sending vehicles direct from depot to depot (see Fig. 6.3).

Consequently the consignment for the Depot 5 region would be sent, along with others originating from the Depot 1 area for distribution in the North West of England, direct to Depot 5 from which they would be despatched to their final destinations.

The first of the two methods described is usually employed by the smaller companies which operate regional distribution policies. This is because they do not usually carry enough goods to justify sending vehicles directly between depots.

If a company which is operating a centralised distribution policy wishes to make the first moves towards a regional system, there are several different ways in which the problem can be approached. It can open a new depot of its own, join forces with an established company based in the area concerned or sub-contract to another company.

The decentralised distribution system also brings with it quite a number of additional financial implications.

A company which owns a number of depots and associated fixed assets will most likely be in a favourable position for attracting more external finance. It can use its property as security for a loan, overdraft or debentures. Owning a lot of property can have its advantages!

One of the aims of decentralisation is to bring about better vehicle utilisation. It is expensive if a vehicle has to return to its depot empty. This system endeavours to avoid empty return journeys. The system should also keep the

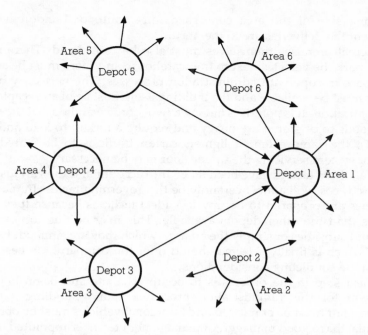

Fig. 6.3 *Regionalised distribution with inter-depot transport. To avoid complication only the connections with Depot 1 are shown but a similar network exists for each depot.*

mileage covered to a minimum. This should result in vast savings in fuel, maintenance and vehicle replacement costs when compared with a centralised system. In simple terms, vehicles should last longer and cost less to run.

Savings should also be possible in manpower. Payments of wages and expenses should be lower as a result of vehicles not being away from their home depot overnight.

Opening a new depot

Once the costing exercises and tests have been completed and the particular company concerned has decided to expand its operation in a particular part of the country by opening a second depot, one of the first variables which must be considered is the actual location of the depot. This can be affected by many factors, each of which must be taken into account in the final choice of situation.

For example, it must be easily accessible. This does not just mean that the gate must be wide enough for an articulated vehicle to enter but that the surrounding roads are of a high standard and within easy reach of other major routes. If this is not the case a lot of time may be wasted on the part of the journey between the main roads and the depot. The geographical situation must also be considered, for it is useless having an ideal depot if it is on the wrong side of the area concerned, e.g. south of London when the majority of the deliveries are to the north.

The actual premises themselves must also be considered. There must be room to park the vehicles next to the warehouse and there must be sufficient office space to cope with administration processes. The necessary handling facilities must be available and the building itself must be of an acceptable size and specification. It is pointless having a two-storey warehouse if the majority of the goods to be stored are heavy and require a forklift to load and unload them. To the same extent if lighter, carton traffic is to be stored then a conveyor system servicing the upper floor may be necessary.

After all these factors have been taken into account and the various options considered, cost will almost certainly be the governing factor. In many cases companies are prepared to occupy less ideal facilities because they actually cost less than the other depots available. This may be due to government grants and subsidies or simply the areas in which they are situated. However, the site which is finally selected should offer the company the best balance between the conflicting considerations.

The next step in the process is to occupy the site and begin operations. Equipment for the administration processes – and handling – must be acquired, staff must be employed and additional vehicles must be obtained. It is essential that a good manager, or management team, is appointed to ensure that everything runs smoothly and efficiently.

The manager must also be capable of obtaining work from the area concerned not only for the depot but also for the other services offered by the company.

It may be necessary to purchase different types of vehicles from those that the company currently uses. For transporting goods between the depots it will almost certainly be more cost-effective to use one large vehicle rather than several smaller ones. Consequently, an articulated vehicle or a large rigid vehicle would probably be best. However, this means that qualified HGV drivers have to be employed and also, possibly, different handling facilities.

The biggest disadvantage of opening a new depot is the extremely high initial cost involved. This is due to obtaining premises and planning permission, employing staff, moving or obtaining vehicles and other equipment, and other associated costs such as advertising the new depot and the resulting changes in the services offered. Unless tight control is maintained the changes do not always increase efficiency and deliveries may in fact take longer. If care is not taken an extra day, or more, could be absorbed by the carriage of the goods between the depots. Consequently, efficient depot staff are essential if the service levels are to be maintained and costs kept down.

If staff are effective and work is obtained from the area surrounding the depot as a result, this can lead to further cost reductions. Normally the larger vehicles which carry the goods from the main depot to the new one would return empty. However, any deliveries destined for the rest of the country, originating from the area around the new depot, would return to the main one on this vehicle, hence reducing the costs which have to be absorbed by each consignment.

One of the principal factors in favour of a company opening a new depot on its own is that it maintains complete control over the whole system. If the company sub-contracts it loses control of factors such as when the goods are actually delivered or where they are stored whilst awaiting delivery. A new depot is simply an extension of the company concerned, so that it can ensure secure warehousing facilities and reliable, satisfactory delivery times. The result is that the quality of service is maintained and customers are kept happy. Also, any profit from work done by the depot remains within the company rather than being given to a sub-contractor.

Joining forces with an established company

An alternative to the high financial outlay of opening a new depot in a particular area is for the company (Company A) to form a working relationship with a similar organisation (Company B) already based there. The idea is that instead of sending several small vans into the area to deliver (as with centralised distribution), Company A would send all the goods to Company B on a larger vehicle. Company B would then deliver the goods using its own fleet of smaller vehicles. Any work which Company B has for the area in which Company A is based would be loaded on to the larger vehicle for the return journey and then delivered by Company A.

This system enables costs to be vastly reduced because the facilities, staff and possibly vehicles are already provided and in operation. If one company does not have enough vehicles but the other has an excess it may be possible to move them to the company which requires them most. This has the added advantage that if, for example, potential customers see the name and address of Company A regularly in Company B's area they may contact Company A for deliveries to their part of the country. They can then be informed of the new service and given the name, address and telephone number of Company B to contact. This should result in more work for both companies. Also, if the new service is promoted it will be easier to obtain work for it through the name of the company based in each area, because they are already established and recognised rather than being seen as a new, risky venture.

A further advantage is that, because the burden of cost is reduced, it is possible for the company hoping to expand to find, and join with, a company better suited to its requirements.

There are several factors which are essential to the success of such a project. First, both companies must enter into the agreement with the same high level of enthusiasm and commitment. Both should strive equally hard to find new work for the service and attempt to give each other as much work as they are receiving. If this is not the case one company will start to think that the relationship is just one-way and that it is giving work away whilst receiving nothing in return. One way to help avoid this is if the agreement is worked on a profit-sharing basis. In this way any profits or losses are shared equally, or according to size or proportion of the business committed to the project.

Consequently, both parties should be encouraged to work hard for their joint success.

It is also necessary to keep a tight control on communication between the two companies to ensure that mistakes are not made due to misunderstandings.

Difficulties may arise if the companies use completely different administration systems, procedures and documentation. This problem is best overcome if the two systems are compared over time, before the new project is put into operation and some agreement reached as to which one of them to adopt.

The biggest problem associated with this system is that, to a certain extent, there is a loss of control over the operation in the other area. This means that when deciding which company to join it is necessary to carry out a very detailed and critical evaluation. The company's service must be examined to determine whether or not its quality, speed and reliability are satisfactory. This includes the security and condition of the facilities, other equipment and the efficiency of the staff and vehicles.

If, for example, the vehicles are all old and in poor condition, e.g. frequent breakdowns resulting in late deliveries, a bad impression will be created with customers which may result in work being lost. Also, if a lot of goods are damaged due to the carelessness of the warehouse staff further problems will arise. Consequently, a thorough and unbiased investigation of all the available options is required if there is to be any chance of the venture succeeding.

Sub-contracting of regional distribution

A further option which involves even less immediate financial outlay is the use of sub-contractors.

In this case the sub-contractor is actually based in the area where the goods are to be delivered rather than in the area from which they originate. The company which holds the contract for the delivery of the goods transports them to the sub-contractor's depot on a large vehicle, hence keeping freight costs low, and the sub-contractor distributes the goods at previously negotiated rates. However, these rates must be sufficiently low to justify using this system.

The biggest disadvantage with the system for the company concerned is that, once the goods are unloaded from the freight vehicle, they are under the complete control of the sub-contractor.

The control of the system and the goods within it is one of the most important factors of a distribution operation. As indicated earlier in this article the greater the control a company wishes to maintain the higher the financial outlay involved.

Conclusion

Whatever has been said about decentralisation is by no means a conclusive argument for its adoption. However, it is clear that this is an area to which management must devote their time and talents. It is most certainly worthy of their consideration. Firms must, however, be big enough to afford to introduce this kind of distribution system. Firms with insufficient resources may link up with another firm in a different area or do a spot of sub-contracting.

There are cost and qualitative benefits. There are also likely to be additional costs, e.g. administration, more complex rehandling costs, insurance of buildings and overheads such as rates, heating, lighting, cleaning, etc.

On the whole, therefore, it is necessary for the company concerned to employ the system which offers what it considers to be the best balance between cost and the other competing factors.

The importance of pricing

Introduction

No price should ever be considered permanent. In fact, far from being final, it is merely a suggestion, or an experiment to test the pulse of the market. If the customer accepts the price, all well and good. However, if it is rejected, the price will either be lowered, or the product withdrawn from the market. The complexity of a company's pricing structure will demand the utmost in capability from management, and before price is determined, an executive should understand both the importance and meaning of price.

Of all the elements of the marketing mix, price is the sole profit generator, the function that provides the profit opportunities, which are either enhanced or diluted in the company's internal operations. Obviously, as such, pricing must produce the right amount of revenue which will cover all costs before there can be a profit. Any other activity in the company becomes academic in profit planning until this primary task has been accomplished.

Pricing determines which products will or will not be sold. As such, pricing should not be given short shrift as an annoying but somehow necessary detail and relegated to the office clerk, unless management is prepared to assign to that individual full responsibility for the effective employment of the company's capital and resources.

In spite of the importance of setting the 'right' price, most companies do not handle pricing well, particularly in service industries. No businessman can price successfully and in depth without a knowledge of his costs, competitive prices, market demand, and ideally, a basis for predicting competitors' behaviour, especially their reaction to price changes. It ought to be possible for a seller of goods and services to fix an optimum price. In attempting to achieve this it is essential that the seller has the right tools, and is familiar with relevant methods, techniques and applications.

Important elements

Back in the 1950s and 1960s, non-price factors grew relatively more important and reached a point where over half a sample of company managers did not select pricing as one of the five most important policy areas in their firm's marketing success. More recently, however, worldwide inflation has again focused attention on price and it is now viewed by many marketers as the most important element of the marketing mix.

Undoubtedly, many of the difficulties associated with price determination and pricing policies start with the rather simple fact that, frequently, we do not really know what we are talking about. Although the concept is quite easy to define, the actual meaning of the word 'price' is little understood. In economic theory, we learn that price, value and utility are related concepts. Utility is the attribute of an item that makes it capable of want satisfaction. Value is the quantitative expression of the power a product has to attract other products in exchange. Because our economy is not geared to a slow barter system, we use money as a common denominator of value and use the term 'price' to describe the money value of an item.

By economic definition, price is the factor which equates supply with demand, which in a competitive environment will tend to settle at a level at which no excess profits are made. It is generally agreed, that whether the theory contains elements of truth or not, it is of no use whatever to the businessman.

Traditionally, price setters considered only a few quite obvious pricing alternatives: keep prices where they are, raise or lower them, and sell now or hold for future sale. Today however, there is much more scope for the creative use of pricing. For example, changes in price can be usefully combined with shifts in advertising, personal sales efforts, promotional activities, and the like. Also, certain prices may be changed whilst keeping others constant.

The more important functions

Perhaps the most important function attributed to price is that of providing signals that call attention to the need for change and thus trigger the desired economic action. However, it would rarely be an increase in price that would lead established firms to expand, it is more likely to be either an increase in demand/orders or a rise in anticipated profitability.

Perhaps the crucial question to be asked is whether higher prices would necessarily lead to higher profit. Sometimes they do, but frequently this is not the case. During the last decade in particular, inflationary pressure has forced costs to rise and prices to go up; the price rise may have been smaller than the cost increase, thus depressing profit margins. Also, at higher prices, less may have been sold, further depressing profits.

It should also be observed that established firms have available to them a reliable signal of a change in demand in the form of varying sales. Sales give a fairly precise indication of the magnitude of the demand increase. In short, prices are, at best, an indirect and unreliable indicator of profit opportunities, and are quite ambiguous signals of changes in demand.

It has already been indicated that prospective profit rather than price, motivates most business decisions, but price changes do perform some useful functions related to motivation.

First, prices are much more public than either profit or profit margins. Secondly, they change more sharply and visibly than actual profits, which respond only after a time lag. As a result, prices do help to inform outsiders that a change in potential profits may be taking place. As such, they are potentially valuable signals.

Obviously generalisations about price cannot apply very widely for a number of reasons:

1 The role of price will vary widely from one sector of the economy to another.

2 Even within the retail and distribution industry, the importance of price to the success of an individual firm differs widely; some firms base their appeal for patronage on low prices while others may use a high price appeal.

3 In some sectors, sellers enjoy considerable latitude as to the choice of price, whilst in others they have almost no discretion. If they do not conform to the prevailing price in the market, they will obtain almost no business.

One often hears business executives talked of as 'a brilliant marketing man', 'a tremendous salesman', but rarely as 'an excellent price-setter'; indeed, very little is known about the participation of senior management in pricing. Further, it is difficult to ascertain, even after the fact, whether most price decisions were 'right', 'wise', or 'well advised'. Outsiders can readily assess the skill and effectiveness of a firm's advertising efforts, sales force, services and the like with considerable confidence, but this doesn't seem to apply when it comes to pricing.

Some executives undoubtedly are far more skilled in setting prices than others, and their skill must affect their firm's profitability.

Dominant factors

According to Oxenfeldt, there are two dominant factors that explain the importance of pricing skill in the success of a firm: the degree of a price-setter's discretion over price and the size of the firm's net profits on sales. Clearly then, to explain the importance of pricing skill, an explanation of the degree of discretion possessed by the price-setter is required. This Oxenfeldt does by means of a matrix (Table 29) which attributes different degrees of price discretion to two factors: similarity of seller's offerings and customer concern for price. It suggests that price discretion is greatest when offerings are highly dissimilar and when customers are mainly concerned with non-price factors.

Table 29: Main determinants of price discretion

Customer concern with price	Similarity of seller's offerings		
	Identical	Modest differences	Large differences
Slight concern	No discretion	Considerable discretion	Great discretion
Moderate concern	No discretion	Modest discretion	Substantial discretion
Overwhelming concern	No discretion	Slight discretion	Slight discretion

Conclusion

In the majority of instances, seller's offerings are dissimilar in some aspects and many customers are quite concerned with price. In such cases then, the firms will occupy a position in which pricing skill will affect profitability very greatly. Thus Oxenfeldt concludes that although the importance of price to a firm's success may be great, this need not mean that it is difficult to set a price.

The pricing of goods and services is a difficult task, but a task that management must devote more time to.

A useful lesson in vfm for the private sector

Savings of £258 million have been made. Opportunities worth around £260 million per year have been identified. And over £100 million could be saved via projects in progress. Such is the value for money experience in the public sector.

Vfm has really taken off in the public sector and around 50 per cent of all auditing resources are now being diverted to this area. But there has tended to be a slow response by the public sector in emulating the private sector in terms of the adoption of management and control techniques.

The three Es of vfm – economy, efficiency and effectiveness – which have enabled dramatic improvements in performance to be achieved in the public sector should be a lesson to the private sector.

There is a great need for the technique to go 'full circle'; that is, developed in the private sector, applied in the public sector and re-applied to the private sector. The time has come for the private sector to emulate the feats of the public sector and to re-launch and re-emphasise vfm.

The private sector can benefit from the three Es:

- *Economy*. To reduce costs in all areas, for example production, marketing, finance, research and development and services, the aim being to prevent wasteful, unrewarding and extravagant expenditure.
- *Efficiency*. Efficient use of resources, for example fixed assets, materials, labour, finance, investments and overheads.
- *Effectiveness*. The realisation of objectives in quantitative and qualitative terms, for example sales targets, profitability, health and safety and so on. This area also covers the sensitive area of reviewing policy decisions and their implementation.

All activities merit consideration. Although a number of activities do receive quite a lot of attention such as the production and marketing functions, vfm in the private sector is still in its infancy. Significant savings are there to be reaped by those companies bold enough to tread the vfm path.

In industry it would appear that a lot of time and effort is devoted towards improving the three Es in the areas of production, marketing, inventory and credit control. But there are areas neglected by past generations which are ripe for vfm investigations:

- *Finance*. There are numerous questions which need to be answered, such as: can the company have a higher plough back of profits? What other sources of finances could have been used and how much would they cost, such as sale and lease back, EEC financing, grants? How about refinancing an existing loan from a lower cost source? Loans once taken out are simply repaid over their life and even though interest rates may fall, refinancing is just never considered.

  Other questions relating to the sources of finance used or to be used would cover alternatives such as the leasing or hire of assets and hire purchase. To make an impact in this area the vfm auditor would need to possess capital-financing skills.

  Most companies make good use of the cashflow forecasting technique (cash budgeting). But many companies do not have any treasury function and so do not earn an adequate return on their short-term surplus cash.

  For large or medium-sized firms it could prove cost-effective to employ a treasurer. For small firms, treasury skills would have to be nurtured in the accounts department.
- *Fixed assets*. In addition to a careful review of the financing of fixed assets, the vfm investigation should ensure that they are being efficiently and effectively used. Why buy machinery, plant or office equipment which just lies idle for most of the time? Idle fixed assets are a waste of scarce resources. Surplus fixed assets need to be identified and disposed of. This creates cash-flow, possibly more space and savings in overheads such as insurance, cleaning and so on.
- *Distribution*. Distribution policy is not always subjected to frequent changes but it is important that it is monitored and reviewed from time to time.

  The vfm appraisal will need to study both quantitative and qualitative data in assessing the three Es. Comparisons and evaluations will have to be made in connection with running costs, various overhead expenses, sub-contracting, contract hire and the quality of service.

- *Research and development.* This is certainly one of the most difficult areas in which to carry out a vfm assignment.

  Hindsight is useful. Past projects could be vetted so as to ensure that mistakes which were made in terms of the three Es are not repeated.

  In the labour area the vfm auditor could look at skill levels required to avoid mundane tasks being carried out by highly skilled, highly paid employees.

  On the equipment side, the review could look at other means of arriving at the same result. Why use hand tools/unsophisticated equipment in the R and D department when the component could be machined in a fraction of the time on the shop floor?

  In the case of materials, provided that the product's function is not impaired, why not use a cheap plastic instead of an expensive brass bar? Also, why build a large expensive prototype when a small model would suffice?

  Whether or not objectives are being met is difficult to determine. But it is a task to which the vfm auditor must address himself.

- *Labour.* There are many labour costs which need to be subjected to detailed examination. The vfm auditor should ensure that overtime is justified and that idle time is unavoidable. Bonus and productivity schemes must be carefully reviewed and monitored.

  From public sector experience, it should be clear that it is possible to make savings in non-productive labour areas such as stores, security, cleaning, canteen and administration. This would involve inter-company comparisons (where possible), the use of temps (for seasonal expansion /contraction), sub-contracting (for example in cleaning, canteen, security services).

  Effectiveness would be particularly important when examining areas such as security services, production control, credit control and inventory control.

- *Overheads.* Management can exercise a considerable amount of influence over this area. Savings can be made even in the areas frequently described as uncontrollable.

  Companies do not do enough shopping around when it comes to insurance, rent and rates.

  While premises, vehicles, public liability and employers' liability have to be insured there is no need to remain with your current insurance company. Companies cannot be moving to new premises every other week, but moving premises could bring about significant savings in rent and rates.

  Energy costs require more thought. Have you ever entered a large retail establishment and been blinded and roasted all in one go?

  Are you getting value for money from your internal and external auditors? Companies can shop around when it comes to their external auditors.

Many companies carry vast stocks of stationery running into thousands of pounds. Orders tend to be made with regular suppliers. It is quite probable that a vfm audit could reveal numerous savings simply by employing a shop around policy. A further vfm task in this area could be to make a study of the stationery inventory control system.

For groups of companies, group purchasing could attract large discounts. This is an area which tends to receive a low priority from a control point of view.

So how can private sector firms implement more effective vfm audits? In the words of Clive Holtham, former finance director for Hammersmith and Fulham: 'Value for money is not simply a part of good management. It is good management.'

Vfm is a management responsibility.

The achievement of the three Es depends upon sound planning, appraisal, authorisation and control systems. Management must ensure that such systems are in operation and working properly.

The personnel who carry out a particular vfm investigation can be either internal or external, or a combination. It should not be assumed that just because a company isn't big enough to employ its own internal audit department, that it cannot use its own members of staff to fulfil vfm duties. Vfm projects are varied and numerous calling for a wide range of skills which the traditional auditor may not possess. Skills, which may exist within one's own organisation.

The vfm function is not so unlike other business functions in that it needs a good information, monitoring and reporting system. There are a number of barriers which tend to limit its progress. A principal barrier is education and training. The vfm auditor requires a really wide range of skills as the work is both of a quantitative and a qualitative nature.

Management are not always willing to succumb to a vfm investigation which looks at the effectiveness of their policies in achieving their objectives. Alternatively, management may not wish to implement the recommendations of the vfm auditor. It may also be difficult to secure the co-operation of the personnel concerned. In the final analysis, it is up to management to manage.

So the benefits of vfm need to be sold to employees via in-company training courses, company employee magazines and suggestion schemes.

Managers must be made responsible for the vfm of their own particular areas. All employees, in addition to accepting the need for vfm must not only cooperate but must also be motivated towards securing its success.

Top management's own policies and objectives need to be subjected to the vfm audit. If UK managerial standards are to improve it is of prime importance that independent vfm performance appraisals take place at regular intervals.

Management have a duty to see that the scarce resources which have been placed at their disposal are used very wisely.

Vfm auditing in the private sector makes good business sense.

Get your priorities right (zero-base budgeting)

More effective resource allocation with zero-base budgeting

A departmental manager said to a colleague, 'We have a budget of £200 000 for plant maintenance this year and so for next year I will be pushing for £250 000.'

At a board meeting one of the directors said, 'If there is no alternative but to cut expenditure in the next financial year, I propose that we have an across-the-board cut and that all our budgets of indirect expenditure be reduced by 5 per cent.'

How often have you heard your own managers/directors say something along these lines? The above statements immediately draw one's attention towards the deficiencies of conventional budgeting. Conventional budgeting does have some effect upon the attitudes of the personnel involved. The question must therefore be asked, 'Is this really the most effective way of allocating scarce resources?'

The departmental manager by his action may ensure that the budget concerned, e.g. plant maintenance, will either keep pace with or ahead of inflation. He will put up a case to support his request for an increased amount. The real question, 'How much should his department really spend on plant maintenance?' remains unanswered and if the truth of the matter were known, in the next financial year £32 000 would have been quite adequate.

Managers and directors who agree to an across-the-board cut in budgets are simply just 'ducking' the issue. The effect of this type of action is that strengths and weaknesses are cut by the same amount when in fact an organisation should be building on its strengths.

Is there an alternative to conventional budgetary control? Yes, Peter A. Phyrr came up with a common-sense approach at Texas Instruments, called Zero-Base Budgeting. *What is zero-base budgeting? How does it work? What is it suitable for?*

It has been found that zero-base budgeting is particularly useful when applied to service and support areas, e.g. research and development, executive training etc. of company activity. However, a company's level of manufacturing activity is determined by its sales volume and thus the production level in turn determines how much the company shall spend on labour, materials and overheads. A decision to increase expenditure for these items does not necessarily bring increased sales although it does tend to boost production volume. Hence there is not the same simple relationship between costs and benefits here as there is in the service and support area. However, it is possible for the zero-base concept to be used in the manufacturing area by making up decision packages to identify alternatives and discretionary activities, allowing management to rank these packages with packages identified for other areas.

ZBB seeks to achieve a more effective allocation of resources in the service and support areas by carefully describing, classifying, sorting and ranking the individual activities concerned.

The basic steps to effective zero-base budgeting are to:

a) Describe each discrete company activity in a 'decision' package.
b) Evaluate and rank all these packages by cost/benefit analysis.
c) Allocate resources accordingly.

When a company applies ZBB it must explain to all levels of management the *decision package concept* and then present guidelines for them to break their area's activities into workable packages. Next, it must set in motion a ranking and consolidation process whereby important packages are identified and given a top rank classification and less important packages are low ranked. This should ease management's task of studying them and making their judgements.

The decision package is a document that identifies and describes a specific activity in such a way that management can:

a) Evaluate it and rank it against other activities competing for the same or similar limited resources, and
b) Decide whether to approve it or disapprove it.

The specifications necessary to the formulation of a successful decision package may include:

a) The objectives of the activity and the means by which those objectives will be achieved.
b) The expected benefits from the programme and the alternatives to the programme.
c) The consequences of not approving the package.
d) The personnel requirements, and
e) Last but not least, the expenditure of funds necessary to carry out the activity.

There are two basic types of decision package:

a) *Mutually exclusive packages* identify alternative means of performing the same function. The best alternative is selected, and the other packages are discarded.
b) *Incremental packages* reflect different levels of effort that may be expended on a specific function. One package, the base package, may establish a minimum level of activity and others identify higher activity levels.

Decision packages are usually formulated at the 'ground level'. This promotes detailed specification of activities and alternatives and generates interest and participation by the managers who will be operationally responsible for the approved budget.

Each manager takes his area's forecasted expense level for the current year, identifies the activities creating this expense and calculates the cost for each activity. He should not try to identify alternatives or increments at this stage.

After he has broken his current operations into preliminary decision packages, he then looks at his requirements for the coming year. To aid him, upper management should issue a formalised set of assumptions on activity

171

levels, wage and salary increases and so on for the coming year. These assumptions not only act as a benchmark for estimating but also act to show up inaccurate assumptions or misunderstandings. They provide a focal point for reviewing and revising assumptions and help everyone keep track of revisions in the list of assumptions and of the changes in activity levels.

The manager translates his packages into 'business as usual packages' for the coming year by costing this year's operations in terms of next year's costs. He then segments his packages into mutually exclusive and incremental packages wherever possible and notes discarded alternatives. If he prefers one of these alternatives to the 'business as usual package', he just swaps the two and develops a set of incremental packages around the new base package. Finally, he should identify all new activities in his area for the coming year and develop decision packages to handle them.

Thus, the manager is then left with a set of packages covering all his activities split into three types:

a) Business as usual packages where he sees no possible or justifiable variations on the level and method of the activity in the package.
b) Decision packages with a base package and incremental packages for all other ongoing activities.
c) Decision packages for new activities.

The ranking process

Having completed the set of packages the manager's next task is to commence the ranking process. The ranking process provides management with a technique with which to allocate its limited resources by ensuring that they concentrate on important questions such as: How much should we spend? and Where should we spend it?

Management may use quantitative or qualitative evaluation techniques in ranking each package giving a higher rank to packages that satisfy minimum operating and legal requirements and a lower rank to the more discretionary packages.

All the packages identified need to be listed in order of decreasing benefit to the company. Management identifies the benefits to be gained at each level of expenditure and studies the consequences of not approving additional decision packages ranked below the expenditure level.

In large companies the number of packages requiring review can reach very large proportions, creating a ponderous if not impossible, task for top management. This dilemma may be resolved by grouping cost centres together naturally, according to the type of activity. The organisational width and depth of such groupings are determined by three factors:

a) The number of packages involved.
b) Local management's ability and willingness to rank unfamiliar activities.
c) The need for extensive review across organisational levels. (This factor is particularly important when deep cuts in expense levels are required to combat poor profits.)

Initial ranking should take place at cost centre level where an individual manager may have enough detailed knowledge of the area concerned to do it himself.

The manager at the next level up the hierarchy reviews all packages passed up and uses cost centre manager rankings as guides to produce a single, consolidated ranking for all packages. As packages move up an organisation the expertise required to rank packages is best provided by a committee rather than an individual. This 'consolidation' hierarchy usually corresponds to the ordinary hierarchical organisation of the company but logical groupings of similar functions may be useful even where these cut across normal organisational boundaries.

Before looking at voting mechanisms, it should be noted that the base package is always ranked higher than the incremental packages clustered around it so that the base can easily be retained even if the increments are rejected. Voting systems may be simple or complex. Three basic schemes are in use:

a) Each member gets one vote on a fixed scale.
b) Each member votes on several different criteria with even or weighted values.
c) A combination of the first two schemes – the first to establish a preliminary ranking and the second to establish a detailed ranking around the cut-off level, after one has been established.

It is helpful to have a review session after detailed ranking has been carried out in which the votes of the members are displayed, misunderstandings of package content and differences of opinion are discussed and a final ranking is established.

Three problems are encountered in the ranking process: firstly, the volume of packages which can be up to several hundreds for a division in a medium-sized company; secondly, managers have conceptual difficulty in ranking packages they consider legally or operationally obligatory and thirdly, concern about their ability to judge the relative importance of dissimilar activities, especially in areas such as staff welfare where almost all packages require subjective evaluation and ranking.

To reduce the number of packages reviewed by higher level management, a cut-off expense line can be established at each organisational level. Management at this level then review in detail and rank only the packages involving expenditure below that cut-off line. Packages above the cut-off line should be briefly reviewed to give management an overall feel for the operation and satisfaction that those packages justify the higher ranking.

It is best to set the cut-off from the very top, estimating the expense that will be approved and setting the cut-off far enough below this expected expense figure to allow the desired trading-off between departments and divisions being ranked. Thereafter, less stringent cut-offs are set at lower consolidation levels (see Fig. 6.4). Thus, management's conceptual difficulty and concern is unfounded, as legally and operationally obligatory packages are highly ranked and only more discretionary packages are looked at in

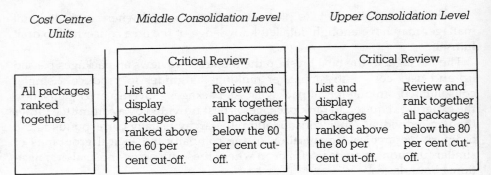

Fig. 6.4 *Zero-base budgeting: the decision ranking cycle*

detail. Furthermore, managers do not concentrate their effort worrying whether package 4 is more important than 5 but that both are more important than package 15 and that in turn is more important than package 25.

The ranked list gives management the means to evaluate the desirability of various expenditure levels throughout the budgeting process. It also provides a reference point in the coming year to identify activities to be reduced or expanded if allowed expenditure levels change.

In conclusion, to quote Peter A. Phyrr, 'ZBB is a flexible and powerful tool. It has greatly simplified the budgeting procedures at Texas Instruments and brought about better resource allocation to boot.'

List of Articles

All of the articles which have been reproduced in this book were written by Leslie Chadwick and his co-authors (as indicated below):

1 Sources of business finance and financial structure
Sources of capital (specially written for this book)

Financial structure
Certified Accountants Students' Newsletter, February 1987

Dividend policy – a practical view
Certified Accountants Students' Newletter, January 1987

The growth of the Venture Capital Market (written jointly with Chris Metalle)
Certified Accountants Students' Newsletter, March 1989

The growth and development of corporate venturing (written jointly with Chris Metalle)
Certified Accountants Students' Newsletter, April 1989

2 The financing of the small business sector
The problems of financing small and medium-sized firms
Certified Accountant, April 1978

Towards a better service for the small business
Accountancy, September 1978

Have the banks failed the small man? (written jointly with David Ward)
Accountancy, March 1982

Are the banks doing enough for small firms? (written jointly with David Ward)
Management Accounting, September 1982

Bank managers – old school or new breed? (written jointly with David Ward)
Journal of the Institute of Bankers, August 1982

Advice and information for small businesses (written jointly with Ken Tonkin)
The Accountant, 10 November 1983

3 Financial analysis
Comparing financial performance – ratio analysis and retail management
Retail and Distribution Management, March/April 1984

Financial analysis revisited: Source data – income measurement
Certified Accountants Students' Newsletter, February 1986

Financial analysis revisited: Source data – the Balance Sheet
Certified Accountants Students' Newsletter, March 1986

Financial analysis revisited: Ratio analysis – a critical appraisal
Certified Accountants Students' Newsletter, April 1986

4   Working capital management
Should we be more inward-looking for that extra finance?
Management Accounting, February 1980

Internal sources of finance: Inventory and debtors
Management Accounting, May 1980

Mail order inventory control (written jointly with Alan Waddington)
Retail and Distribution Management, March/April 1983

The costs of holding stocks
Management Services, October 1982

The reduction of inventory holding costs
Management Services, November 1982

Materials management, profitability and the construction industry
Building Technology & Management, February 1982

Mail order profitability (written jointly with Alan Waddington)
Retail & Distribution Management, November/December 1981

Credit Control – Mail order: A risky return (written jointly with Alan Waddington)
The Accountant, 11 February 1982

Devising a sound creditor policy (written jointly with Keith Pickles)
Management Accounting, March 1988

Buried treasure
Journal of the Institute of Bankers, October 1980

Generation of internal finance by Production Management
Management Accounting, July/August 1980

The role of Marketing in internal finance
Management Accounting, February 1981

The accountant and marketing management (written jointly with J. Ratnatunga)
The Accountant, 17 November 1983

5   Capital investment appraisal
Capital investment appraisal – Which discount rate?
Certified Accountants Students' Newsletter, March 1987

Capital investment and the tax factor
Certified Accountants Students' Newsletter, December 1986

Money doesn't mean everything: The non-financial aspects of capital investment appraisal
Accountants Weekly, 12 June 1981

The planning and evaluation of capital investments
Extract from Management and Control of Capital in Industry (written jointly with Prof. Richard Pike), CIMA, 1985

6 Other issues

The financial aspects of centralised distribution (written jointly with Duncan Aspinall)
Management Accounting, July/August 1985

The financial aspects of decentralised distribution (written jointly with Duncan Aspinall)
Management Accounting, October 1985

The importance of pricing (written jointly with Deborah Rogers)
The Accountant, 12 July 1984

A useful lesson in vfm for the private sector
Accountancy Age, 9 October 1986

Get your priorities right (zero base budgeting) (written jointly with Bruce Thew)
Certified Accountants Students' Newsletter, October 1986

Index